AVID

READER

PRESS

ALSO BY TOMMY TOMLINSON

The Elephant in the Room:
One Fat Man's Quest to Get
Smaller in a Growing America

DOGLAND

PASSION, GLORY,
and Lots of **SLOBBER** *at the*
WESTMINSTER DOG SHOW

Tommy Tomlinson

AVID READER PRESS

NEW YORK LONDON TORONTO SYDNEY NEW DELHI

AVID READER PRESS
An Imprint of Simon & Schuster, LLC
1230 Avenue of the Americas
New York, NY 10020

First Avid Reader Press hardcover edition April 2024

AVID READER PRESS and colophon are trademarks of Simon & Schuster, LLC

Simon & Schuster: Celebrating 100 Years of Publishing in 2024

For information about special discounts for bulk purchases, please contact Simon &
Schuster Special Sales at 1-866-506-1949 or business@simonandschuster.com.

The Simon & Schuster Speakers Bureau can bring authors to your live event. For
more information or to book an event contact the Simon & Schuster Speakers
Bureau at 1-866-248-3049 or visit our website at www.simonspeakers.com.

Interior design by Ruth Lee-Mui
Photo credit page iv: UPI / Alamy Stock Photo

Manufactured in the United States of America

1   3   5   7   9   10   8   6   4   2

Library of Congress Cataloging-in-Publication Data

Names: Tomlinson, Tommy, author.
Title: Dogland : passion, glory, and lots of slobber at the
Westminster Dog Show / Tommy Tomlinson.
Identifiers: LCCN 2024000817 (print) | LCCN 2024000818 (ebook) |
ISBN 9781982149321 (hardcover) | ISBN 9781982149338
(paperback) | ISBN 9781982149345 (ebook)
Subjects: LCSH: Tomlinson, Tommy. | Westminster Kennel Club. Dog Show. |
Dog shows—New York (State)—New York. | Show dogs—United States. |
Journalists—United States—Biography. | BISAC: PETS / Dogs / General |
BIOGRAPHY & AUTOBIOGRAPHY / Entertainment & Performing Arts
Classification: LCC SF425.16.N72 N487 2024 (print) | LCC SF425.16.N72
(ebook) | DDC 636.7/0811097471—dc23/eng/20240122
LC record available at https://lccn.loc.gov/2024000817
LC ebook record available at https://lccn.loc.gov/2024000818

ISBN 978-1-9821-4932-1
ISBN 978-1-9821-4934-5 (ebook)

For Alix, always

And this time, for Fred

Contents

God creates the world and say on Saturday afternoon he must separate the animals from man, so he creates a sudden chasm like an earthquake that leaves man on one side and the animals on the other. And while the chasm's open, dog jumps over and stands by man. And that's the way it's gonna be. That's the way it's gotta be.

—Barry Hannah

Bow wow wow yippee yo yippee yay
Bow wow yippee yo yippee yay.

—George Clinton, "Atomic Dog"

Prologue

Are those dogs happy?

That thought formed in my head one night years ago as I watched the Westminster Dog Show on TV. The way I remember it, I actually cocked my head, like a curious spaniel.

Dogs, I loved. Dog shows? They always seemed a little strange. Westminster was the only one I'd ever paid attention to, and I knew just two things about it. One, it was the pinnacle of the dog-show world, like Wimbledon or the Super Bowl. And two, it pissed me off every year because it preempted *Monday Night RAW* on the USA Network. I always forgot it was coming. I'd tune in to see "Stone Cold" Steve Austin and end up watching a Shih Tzu. Plus, the dogs didn't *do* anything. They definitely didn't do anything they were bred to do. Instead, dog after dog—little dogs meant to catch rats, medium dogs built to hunt birds, giant dogs made to pull sleds or guard castles—pranced around a show ring, accompanied by handlers wearing either the blandest outfits possible or something from the Elton John collection.

Like a lot of people, I love the 2000 dog-show mockumentary *Best in Show*. I still laugh at Christopher Guest naming nuts. I can hum the chorus to "God Loves a Terrier." I also figured there was some truth to it, enhanced for comic effect, the way *This Is Spinal Tap* both made fun of and showed fondness for its aging heavy metal band. But I didn't think any deeper about dog shows than that. Not until that text from the ether lodged in my brain.

Are those dogs happy?

And before I could process that one, another question arrived: *Are regular dogs happy, too?*

I have spent my life around dogs. Even when I didn't own one, I had buddies or girlfriends or family members who did. My wife and I had nearly fifteen years with a yellow Lab mutt named Fred. You will meet him a little later on. I've been bitten twice: once by the neighbor's German shepherd when I was six or seven years old, and the second time a few years ago by a new friend's dog when I absentmindedly pulled its head out of the kitchen trash. I've met dogs I didn't like. I've been afraid of a dog now and then. But I've fallen in love with about 95 percent of the dogs I've ever met. And part of the reason is that those dogs acted like they loved me.

I say "acted like." Because the truth is, we only think we know.

A dog will wag and lick your face and just about knock the door down waiting for you to come in at the end of the day. But are they *really* thrilled? Or are they running the world's longest con, a scheme developed over thousands of generations for better chow and a warm place to sleep?

And what, exactly, do *we* get out of the deal? What is it about the bond between people and dogs that makes so many people weep harder for a dying dog than they do for a member of their own human family? (If you can't bear the death of a dog *even in a movie*, there's a website for you: doesthedogdie.com.)

We've taught dogs to shake hands and roll over and catch a Frisbee with their teeth. But somehow, along the way, they've also learned to make a deep emotional connection with human beings. It's their greatest trick—so good that a lot of human beings can't pull it off. How do dogs do it?

All those lingering questions led to this book. And this book led me to travel around the country, going from dog shows at midwestern fairgrounds to Madison Square Garden. There is a whole hidden world out there, a roaming carnival of dogs and their people that most of us rarely glimpse. Somewhere in America, this very weekend, a convention center or municipal auditorium or livestock arena near you has been converted into a four-day pageant of pointers and Pomeranians, along with the people who groom and show and judge them. In any subculture there are some people who are enthusiasts and some who are obsessives. The dog-show world has plenty of both.

Beyond the ring, there's another world of researchers who spend their lives in the fast-growing practice of dog studies. It's part of a relatively new field called anthrozoology—the study of the relationships between humans and other animals. Scientists all over the world are trying to get a better sense of what dogs think and feel, and how they interact with us. They are slowly closing the distance between what we thought we knew about dogs and what we really know.

The volume of information on dogs is overwhelming. Every day, my dog-show Google alerts unroll like a CVS receipt. I've got a bookshelf full of dog books and a phone full of dog podcasts.

But I'm still an amateur compared with nearly all the other people you'll meet in this book. My goal is not to be an expert—no chance of that. My goal is to tell you what it's like out there in Dogland.

Dogland. That's what I started calling it, after going to dozens of dog shows over nearly three years. In my mind I started to think of them as one big show—an immense and portable theme park of dogs.

But our relationship with dogs covers a much more vast span of time and space. We've been hanging with dogs, and they've been hanging with us, for thousands upon thousands of years. They have become our roommates, our playmates, our soulmates. From the moment we started leaning on each other, we have changed dogs' lives in countless and profound ways. And they have changed ours.

Are dogs really happy?

Somewhere in the answer to that question, I thought, might be the secret to our happiness, too.

A Word on Bitches

Heads up: in the pages that follow, you are going to encounter the word "bitch."

Like, a *lot*.

The point of dog shows, at least in theory, is to identify the best male and female dogs for breeding. Gender is everything. So people at dog shows throw around "bitch" like it's nothing.

At a dog show, you will hear "bitch" over the PA system and see it repeatedly in the official program. In most breed competitions, male and female dogs start out competing separately. The best female dog is called the Winners Bitch. Below that is a category called Select Bitch, which means—well, here's a description from an American Kennel Club (AKC) guide: "The Select Bitch is similar to Awards of Merit in that this bitch is the next best as far as the quality of the Bitches in competition."

That's three bitches in one sentence. Triple bitch points.

(A generic male dog, by the way, is just . . . a dog. We need a semi-vulgar word for a male dog to even things out. Maybe a really good male dog could be the Select Prick.)

Once you start looking, "bitch" is everywhere at dog shows. A dog handler's assistant—the person who, for example, fills the dogs' food and water bowls—is often called a "bucket bitch." That applies to the guys, too. There's no such thing as a "bucket bastard."

A recent issue of *Showsight*, one of the dog-show trade magazines, featured an article on breeding called "The Foundation Bitch." The Dog Museum of America, a precursor to the current AKC Museum of the Dog, once held a needlework exhibition called *Bitches in Stitches*.

One day, combing through old online posts, I came across a spectacular sentence on a blog by a woman who writes about her adventures with show dogs: "Today Carolyn gave Dolly a blow job before she went into winners—well done—and Dolly was Winners Bitch!" (I am fairly certain "blow job" refers to the dog getting its hair styled. But however you visualize that sentence is up to you.)

The word "bitch" has existed in one form or another for more than a thousand years, and it's been a slur aimed at women since around the year 1400. Some women (and some gay men) have reclaimed the word for themselves. It's become one of those words you can use if you're in the group, but not if you're on the outside—sort of like how I can say something about my mama, but *you* better not say something about my mama.

I would never call a woman a bitch. I do, from time to time, say "son of a bitch"—most often when I kick the bedpost at three in the morning, or when the Carolina Panthers fumble at the goal line. I rationalize that I'm not really saying "bitch," but I am, of course—just one step removed.

I've spent several years in the dog-show world now, and I'm still not comfortable saying "bitch" by itself. My interview transcripts all have me stumbling around and saying something like "uh, you know, female dog." I'd feel more at ease having the book read like that. But it wouldn't be true to this world and the people in it.

There's a clip from Westminster 2017 you can find online. A Norwegian elkhound named Duffy has just won the Hound Group, and the TV interviewer asks the judge, Polly Smith, why she picked Duffy. Smith has a simple answer: "This bitch epitomizes type in a Norwegian elkhound."

The crowd at Madison Square Garden busts out laughing. But Smith doesn't laugh until the crowd noise bounces back to her. It takes her a second to realize the audience thought she was saying something outrageous. She wasn't. She was just talking how dog people talk. And that's what this book is going to sound like. No sense bitching about it.

How a Dog Show Works

Round 1

Dogs compete only against other dogs from the same breed. A judge picks one winner as Best of Breed.

(As of 2022, the American Kennel Club recognized two hundred breeds as eligible for dog shows.)

Round 2

Breed winners compete in seven groups, with typically twenty-five to thirty-five dogs in each group:

- **Herding:** Dogs designed to move other animals along. Examples: German shepherds, border collies, Old English sheepdogs.
- **Hound:** Dogs bred to track and hunt. Examples: basset hounds, dachshunds, Rhodesian ridgebacks.
- **Non-Sporting:** A catchall group for dogs that don't fit other categories. Examples: bulldogs, Dalmatians, standard poodles.

- **Sporting:** Generally, bird dogs. Examples: Labrador retrievers, cocker spaniels, English setters.
- **Terrier:** Self-explanatory. Examples: Airedales, Scottish terriers, wire fox terriers.
- **Toy:** Smaller breeds. Examples: Chihuahuas, Pekingese, pugs.
- **Working:** Guard dogs, sled dogs, rescue dogs. Examples: boxers, Great Danes, Saint Bernards.

Round 3

The seven group winners compete for Best in Show.

1

SHOW QUALITY

Sherlock Holmes was right. It is a curious thing when the dogs do not bark.

I'm walking across a massive lawn on the banks of the Hudson River, about an hour north by train from Grand Central Station. Up ahead is a gigantic canopy with purple flags. That's where the dogs are. This is the last day of the 2022 Westminster Dog Show, the most famous and important dog show in the world, the only dog show most Americans have ever heard of. More than three thousand dogs from two hundred breeds entered this Westminster. Most of them have been knocked out by now. By the end of the day there will be only one.

As anyone who works for Westminster will tell you, often repeatedly, it is the second-longest-running annual sporting event in American history, behind only the Kentucky Derby. For its first 144 years, Westminster was a New York City event, a February tradition at Madison Square Garden. But in 2021, COVID drove

the show outdoors. It landed up here in Tarrytown at the Lyndhurst estate. Lyndhurst is a National Historic Landmark—sort of
a Biltmore House of the North. It used to belong to Jay Gould,
the old robber baron. In the post–Civil War era, Gould tried to
control both the gold market and the railroad industry. Neither
play worked, but he accumulated more than $2 billion in today's
dollars along the way. Lyndhurst—sixty-seven acres of sprawling
parkland anchored by a Gothic mansion—wasn't even Gould's
primary home. Just his summer getaway.

The Goulds were also dog people; Jay's son Frank bred Saint
Bernards here at Lyndhurst in a two-story kennel. But the connection goes deeper. This feels like a place where a dog show should
be. Status and excess are baked into dog shows and have been
from their very beginnings. Westminster gives off the sheen of
wealth even though most of the people involved in dog shows are
not wealthy. Westminster awards no prize money at all. The Best
in Show winner this year gets a pewter trophy, a Steuben crystal
bowl, an eight-by-ten-inch picture frame, a sterling silver cup, and
what can best be described as a big-ass ribbon. At most shows, a
champion's haul is often just the fancy ribbon and a sack of dog
food. Champion dogs do generate breeding fees for their owners,
but there's no serious money in it, the way there is in horse racing.
Dog shows are less about the prizes than about the aspirations
pulsing underneath. The breathtaking Lyndhurst lawn, slowly
sloping down to the river, serves as both a Jay Gatsby fantasy and
the field of a dog's dreams.

Just not these dogs. At least not today. They're at work.

I reach the edge of the tent and close my eyes. I hear genera-
tors, golf carts, the whine of hair dryers. Every so often there is

applause from a distant corner, like the cheers on a faraway hole at a golf tournament. Eventually I can make out conversations among the dog people: the handlers, the judges, the fans. Tonight the show will move to an indoor tent, which has been set up with bleachers and lit for prime time. But in these early stages, everybody mingles.

You can get close to a show dog, even pet it if the handler says it's OK. A handler spelled out the rules for me early on. Ask for permission first. Don't pet the dog on top of its head—that fur has been combed and sprayed and maybe powdered a little to shine up the coat. Instead, go for the scritch under the chin. Don't be surprised to come away with a schmear of slobber on your hand. You can train a dog to do many things, but you can't teach it not to drool.

A good dog, to humans, is a dog that does what we want it to do. This, of course, is not always what the dog wants to do. Left on their own, most would spend their days licking their crotches and rolling in roadkill. And even though a few breeds are naturally silent, most dogs vocalize. Dogs growl at the UPS truck, moan with loneliness, whimper in fear, yap at a rival, bellow at the injustice of the world. (That last one is a guess.) To live with a dog is to occasionally wish the dog would shut the hell up.

But these dogs are as quiet as Buckingham Palace guards. They have been trained for this. Most of them have spent nearly their whole lives either at dog shows or traveling to them. It's impossible to know what they are thinking, even though a huge part of our relationship with dogs is that we *think* we know what they're thinking. Here's what I think they're thinking right now, here at the dog show: *This is no longer worth barking about.*

Eight show rings, each about half the size of a basketball court, circle the giant canopy. All eight rings are going at once. In Ring 6 a handler named Laura King is bent down over a white dog, whispering in his ear, as they wait for the breed competition to start.

Laura—blond-streaked hair, skirt set, sensible black shoes—will turn fifty-two the month after the show. She's sharp and funny outside the ring, soothing and skilled inside it. She tends to talk in clichés when the cameras are on her but seems incapable of being anything but herself otherwise. She wanted to be a dog handler from the time she was seven years old. Not including college and a brief career in accounting, it's all she's ever done.

She is prone to roll her eyes at pretense and bullshit, both of which dog shows have in abundance. But she loves the work deeply and the dogs profoundly, so she puts up with the rest. Nearly every weekend, she and her longtime partner, Robin Novack—also a dog handler and an expert breeder—traipse from their home in Illinois to a dog show somewhere, hauling crates of dogs, a couple of assistants, and a jug of margarita mix. Laura is in high demand—at this Westminster, she is showing seventeen dogs. But this dog in Ring 6 is different. The assistants don't work with this one. Laura handles him alone.

He is the rough shape and size of a husky, a solid midsize dog, but it's the fur you notice: a spectacular white coat fluffed out until it blurs to silver at the edges. He looks like a walking snowbank. He's a Samoyed, formally pronounced *SAM-uh-yed*, although most people say it *suh-MOY-ed*. The breed dates back more than three thousand years, to a nomadic Siberian tribe called the Nenets. The Nenets were once called *samo-yed*, a Russian phrase that, depending on the translation, might have been a slur meaning "cannibal." (Nenets just means "man." The tribe upgraded their name and left the dog with the old one.) The Nenets bred Samoyeds to pull sleds and herd reindeer. This particular dog has never seen a reindeer and has never mushed. But in his world he is the greatest Samoyed of all time. He has won 111 Best in Shows. He's one of the most decorated dogs in North American history. *The Canine Chronicle*, one of the dog-show trade magazines, ranked him as the top dog in the country in 2021. That year, in Westminster's first show at Lyndhurst, he made the final group of seven.

I have held off on telling you his name because this will take a minute. Show-dog names are ridiculous. There are no Rovers or Fifis at dog shows. Instead there is a constant contest to see who can go the most over the top. A show dog's first name is generally the name of the kennel where it was born. The breeder or owner adds on to that, often with some elaborate phrasing based on a pun or a song or an inside joke. It's gotten so out of hand that the American Kennel Club, the oldest and largest dog registry, limits a dog's official name to fifty characters. Among the dogs at this Westminster:

Wishing Well Bobcat's Peace, Love & Pixie Dust

Ides of March Runs with Scissors

Delamer Suzi Sells Sushi on the Boardwalk

BeeCreeks Evenkeel You're Gonna Need a Bigger Boat

You get the idea. Like Mad Libs, except the sentences make no sense.

Beyond the names, a champion dog accumulates titles like a British royal. Every dog at Westminster has at least a CH, for "champion," and many have GCH, for "grand champion." They earn titles for various other achievements, some of which are recognized by the AKC and others that are more like a celebrity's honorary doctorate.

All of that leads to this: the Samoyed in the ring with Laura is officially named—deep breath now—MBIS MBISS CAN GCH AM GR CHP Vanderbilt 'N Printemp's Lucky Strike.

Nobody, of course, calls him that. Like every show dog, he also has a call name—the name he actually answers to.

He goes by Striker.

Striker exists because of an event that sounds like a sentence from a Mötley Crüe tour diary: his mother, a bitch named Cherry Brandy, flew to Denmark to mate with a stud named Happy Go Lucky.

Both parents were champion show dogs. Brandy flew back to the States and gave birth to three puppies—all boys—on June 4, 2015. The moment the puppies were born, the clock started ticking toward the decision that would set the course of their lives.

Technically, dogs in dog shows are not competing against one another. They're supposed to be judged by how close they come to the "breed standard"—a set of guidelines, written by that breed's official club, that describes how that dog should look and act. The Best in Show winner is supposed to be the dog that hews the closest to its breed standard—the most perfect version of itself. It's as if humans decided that George Clooney was the consummate man, and we measured all other men by which ones were the Clooneyest.

Dogs grow fast, and their lives as show dogs last just a few years, so breeders have to decide early which puppies have a chance to fill out into the breed standard. Picking a top show dog is like drafting an NFL quarterback when they're still in elementary school. Some breeders are superstitious about exactly when they evaluate the litter: a certain number of days after birth, or a certain time of the morning, or a certain phase of the moon. Anything to tip the odds on what is mostly an educated guess.

A Canadian breeder named Judi Elford, owner of a kennel called Vanderbilt Samoyeds, co-owned Brandy with a Delaware breeder named Mengru Wu. Three and a half months after the litter was born, the two women met in Fineview, New York—a convenient place for Judi to bring the puppies across the border. As they evaluated the puppies together, Judi kept coming back to the same one. He had the right build, and he walked with a smooth gait—what she calls an "easy mover." But beyond that, he had a strong personality. He locked eyes with whoever was watching him. He wanted attention and gave it back. He was drawn to people and Judi was drawn to him. So she claimed him. Judi keeps a running list of potential dog names. One of them was Lucky Strike, which felt natural because the puppy's father was Happy Go Lucky. When she added in the names of the parents' two kennels, she ended up with Vanderbilt 'N Printemp's Lucky Strike. Striker for short.

Mengru chose one of the other two puppies to develop as a show dog. She and Judi decided the third puppy did not quite measure up. In the dog breeding world, the first two puppies were "show quality." The third was "pet quality."

Pet-quality puppies end up with regular families—well, regular families who can afford a purebred dog. They go on to live what we think of as a normal dog's life.

Show-quality dogs enter a different world.

Instead of learning to fetch a Frisbee, a show dog learns to hold a stack—the still, wide-legged pose a dog is supposed to hold while the judge is watching. Instead of scarfing table scraps, a show dog eats carefully calibrated meals and takes supplements for stronger teeth and a shinier coat. There's an even longer list of what a show dog has to learn *not* to do: Do not automatically sniff another dog's butt. Do not run off when you see a squirrel. Do not flinch, if you are a male dog, when a judge comes up from behind and checks your testicles. Show dogs are intended to provide pure-bred breeding stock. A male show dog has to be double-balled and ready to go.

(I feel obligated to inform you here about the existence of a product called Neuticles, which are silicone testicles for neutered dogs. Needless to say, at Westminster a set of Neuticles would be an automatic DQ.)

One final rule: Don't bark when it's showtime.

This has been Striker's whole life. Now, here in Ring 6, his Westminster is about to begin.

Laura is tense but he is not. He bows to her in the classic downward-dog pose: *Let's play!* She reaches down and cuffs his chin.

Striker's first hurdle is the breed competition. There are twenty-six Samoyeds competing in this round. They form a crowded oval in the ring. The dogs are just a couple of feet apart but pay almost no attention to one another. Their handlers hold them close. Most show dogs don't wear a traditional collar or leash. Their handlers use a lead, pronounced like *need*. The most basic lead is a thin strip of nylon cord with a ring on one end. You run the other end through the ring, and it makes a loop that goes around the dog's neck. A smart dog can slip out of a lead, and a stubborn one can pull until it chokes. It's not a tool for an impatient dog. So much of a dog show is waiting. Short walks interrupted by long pauses. Golf without the clubs. But Striker doesn't struggle against the lead. By now he knows what comes next.

"No matter how good physically a dog is, if they don't have the heart to do it, it won't matter," Laura told me once. "What we do here can be very grueling. I'm exhausted and I *know* what's going on. He's happy to be out there every time. He's just really enthusiastic when he goes out there, and you can tell he's loving what he's doing. He's loving his life and it shows."

It does show. There is some strange essence about Striker that sets him apart, even in a group of dogs that look pretty much just like him. Call it a vibe. Watch him for a minute or two and you get the sense he'd be a great hang—playful, confident, upbeat. Every dog at Westminster is among the prime of its breed. They all look like they're supposed to look and walk like they're supposed to walk. A big part of the difference is how much they seem to enjoy it. When I first went to dog shows, I had no clue which dogs would win. But after a while I could pick out a dog from the crowd and usually be right. I hadn't suddenly developed a trained eye for the proper muzzle length. I just noticed that some dogs can create joy out of nothing and the joy is transferable. Striker has the vibe. He is good enough for Best in Show. And Best in Show at Westminster is the world heavyweight championship.

The breed competition is starting at 11 a.m.; if Striker wins that, he'll compete against the rest of the Working Group in the TV tent around 8 p.m. And if he wins *that*, the Best in Show round won't start until around 10:30 p.m., and they won't announce the winner until just before eleven. That is a long-ass day for a dog and even more so for a human. Laura didn't get much sleep the night before. She doesn't care. She has never showed a dog that won Westminster. Striker might be the best chance she'll ever have.

Show quality or pet quality, dogs don't get to choose their lives. This is the path Striker's people chose for him. Tying themselves to him is the path they have chosen for themselves. They are bound for the mystery together.

The judge splits the Samoyeds into smaller groups so they don't crowd the ring. Laura and Striker are part of the first group to show. Traditionally, each dog-and-handler pair starts by taking a lap around the ring. Laura and Striker head out at their practiced pace, counterclockwise, side by side. The lead is taut between them. It is hard to tell who is leading who.

Here is how scientists think it might have happened, somewhere between fifteen thousand and thirty thousand years ago:

Humans of that era were mainly hunters traveling in camps. They made fire and ate meat by the fire. The cooking meat attracted wolves who were drawn to the aroma but stayed safely out of range. Every so often a human would fling a bone into the darkness. The wolves gnawed on the bones. They trailed the humans to the next campsite, still keeping their distance. Over time there was an unspoken arrangement. The humans made sure the wolves ate well, and the wolves alerted the humans to intruders.

Over time the wolves crept closer. One fateful night a curious wolf came all the way into the light of the fire. The humans didn't chase it off. Slowly, the humans mingled with the wolves. And at some point—days or months or generations later—a wolf curled up at a human's feet. Maybe got its belly rubbed. That was the first dog.

There are other theories. Biologist Raymond Coppinger came up with the "garbage dump" scenario, where wolves gathered around the trash piles humans made when they started to settle into villages. Some wolves didn't run when humans approached the garbage dump, and eventually those wolves evolved into dogs. They basically created themselves.

Other scholars believe humans played a more active role from the beginning, maybe as far as taking weaned wolf pups from their dens and raising them. There's even some thought that human mothers fed the cubs with their own breast milk. (That inverts the myth of Romulus and Remus, the twin brothers who suckled a she-wolf before Romulus killed his twin and founded the city of Rome.)

Dogs are some of the most diverse creatures on Earth. They include everything from the tiniest teacup Chihuahua to the most massive Leonberger (AKC description: "a lush-coated giant"). But every dog that has ever existed evolved from the wolf—specifically, most scientists believe, the gray wolf. (A competing theory says a now-extinct species of wolf was the dog's true ancestor.) Many researchers believe dogs originated in east Asia. Some think a different type of dog evolved around the same time in Europe. There is evidence to support several competing theories on how, where, when, and why dogs came to be. But it is still mostly a mystery.

Clearly, *something* happened out there. The wolves that hung out with humans began to morph inside and out. They developed shorter muzzles and smaller teeth. Their instinct to run became a desire to stay close. As far as we can tell, dogs are the first animals that humans ever tamed. And once we learned it was possible, humans tamed other animals—goats, sheep, horses—and eventually the very land around them. Dogs enabled restless humans to stay put. They helped humans create societies built around the homestead instead of the hunt.

We domesticated dogs, and they domesticated us.

At some point in all this change, humans realized dogs could be even more useful if they didn't mate at random but were bred with a purpose—pairing the strongest male and female, for instance, in hopes of creating more powerful offspring. Again, the fossil record is blurry. Some scientists think this happened some nine thousand years ago, in the same general area of Siberia where the Samoyed would later come from. What's more clear is that as humans migrated and mingled, dogs spread across the world, and people needed them for different jobs. Those human needs required dogs of different shapes and sizes and temperaments, so early breeders experimented until they created a dog that could do the work they wanted.

In seventeenth-century Germany, for example, the problem was badgers: toothy little assholes that destroyed lawns, ate farmers' crops, and spread disease. When chased, they retreated into burrows that were too small for farm dogs to get inside. So breeders, starting with a pinscher and a miniature pointer, developed the dachshund (literally, "badger dog" in German). Dachshunds are long and narrow, with short, powerful legs. They were built to dive into a hole, clamp onto a badger, and drag it out. They have a unibrow of bone to protect their eyes from claws, and a strong curved tail in case the owner had to pull out dog and badger both. Today they're considered one of the crankier breeds. Now you see why.

(During World War I, some Americans called dachshunds "liberty hounds" to erase their Germanness. I suspect the dogs would not have cared. They had been through worse.)

Beyond the AKC-approved breeds, there are dozens more unofficial breeds—not random mutts, but crossbreeds developed for one purpose or another. Some of the most popular dogs in America are crossbreeds like the Labradoodle. Wally Conron, an Australian breeder, created the Labrador-poodle mix in the '80s as a guide dog for a blind woman whose husband was allergic to dog fur. He wishes he hadn't. "I find that the biggest majority are either crazy or have a hereditary problem," he told the *New York Times* in 2019.

The president of the Australian Labradoodle Club of America had this rebuttal: "All dogs are crazy."

Fair.

What I take from that story is how it started: a guy saw a problem and built a dog to solve it. This is the essential quality of dogs. They are the greatest multi-tool ever created, endlessly versatile, able to adapt to an astonishing range of human needs—including the need for a dog in the first place. If the scientific theories are correct, dogs would not exist if not for us. We are their god.

It is also easy to imagine a past where humans couldn't survive without dogs as servants and protectors. Around the time early humans evolved, Neanderthals also walked the planet. At some point—roughly forty thousand years ago—humans started to thrive at the time Neanderthals died off. Somewhere in there is also when a branch of the gray wolf began to evolve into the dog. Some scientists believe the timing is not a coincidence. Maybe having dogs was the key advantage that kept humans going. It doesn't take much of a leap to think that the dog is our savior.

Either way, dogs and humans are completely connected. The tracks of their histories run side by side. The leash pulls from both ends.

Our connection to dogs is buried deep inside our very language. If someone's the best, they're the top dog; but if they're underperforming, they're dogging it. (Somewhere in between, talented but arrogant, are the ones hotdogging it.) If you want to save tasty morsels from a restaurant, you get a doggie bag, but a bunch of haphazard scraps are a dog's breakfast. You work like a dog, in a dog-eat-dog world, and go home dog-tired. If that causes you to drink too much and get sick as a dog, the morning cure is hair of the dog. You can start the day running with the big dogs and end the day in the doghouse. The only comfort is that every dog has his day. As long as you don't let the tail wag the dog.

Sometimes a dog stands for something undefinable but undeniable. Just about the highest praise a ballplayer can give a teammate is that he's "got that dog in him," or even better, "got that dawg in him." ("Dawg" being a cooler, tougher version of "dog." You can most definitely go down a rabbit hole of how "dog" morphed into "dawg." I do not recommend it.) The phrase is so omnipresent that college football writer Rodger Sherman tweeted in 2022:

if ESPN wants to be the continued broadcaster of every sports
draft they need to have someone on the desk issuing a ruling on
whether that player does or does not Have That Dog In Him

Whenever an athlete has a great game, someone on social
media will pair the phrase with a photoshopped X-ray of a torso
with a dog inside. The dog always looks like it's wondering how
the hell it got inside somebody's chest cavity.

This all leads to one of the great memes in Internet history.
It involves the 2000 movie *Finding Forrester*, which stars Rob
Brown as a Black teenager named Jamal Wallace, who is not just
a basketball star but an aspiring writer. Through some convoluted
movie stuff, he ends up meeting and befriending a reclusive, J. D.
Salinger–esque novelist named William Forrester. Drama ensues.
The climax involves a championship basketball game *and* an essay
contest. Forrester finally leaves his apartment. The day is saved.

I am telling you all this for two reasons. One is that William
Forrester is played by Sean Connery. And the second is that Connery, as Forrester, says this line to Jamal in a key scene:

"You're the man now, dog!"

I wish print could properly convey how hilarious this line
sounds coming from the mouth of a seventy-year-old Scottish actor
who is playing a seventy-year-old Scottish novelist speaking to a
Black teenager. Instead of saying, "You're the *man* now, dog"—
the way anyone who had ever heard the phrase before would say
it—he chooses to say, "You're the man *now*, dog." To this day I
can't decide if this is the work of an out-of-touch white guy, or a
famous actor's brilliant portrayal of an out-of-touch white guy.

Either way, for the next five years or so, that clip was

unavoidable on social media. The ironic use of "dog" as a compliment outstripped the actual compliment for a while. It was another example of the dog's extraordinary flexibility as a literary device. We can make "dog" mean pretty much whatever we want it to mean.

We can also make "sporting event" mean pretty much what we want it to mean. As I mentioned earlier, Westminster bills itself as the second-oldest continuously held sporting event in American history. This depends a lot on what you consider to be a "sporting event." Is Westminster a competition? Yes. Are there winners and losers? Yes. Is there some kind of physical activity involved? Yes. Are there teams? Yes. Do all the teammates *know* they're in a competition?

Hmm.

We allow ourselves to believe so many things about dogs. Believing they care about winning or losing a dog show feels like a very small leap. It's like watching a magic trick. It makes it so much easier if you choose to believe in magic.

The judge of the Samoyed breed competition is Rick Gschwender, pronounced *GISH-WEN-der*. He's a retired electrician for Ford who has the slick grayish hair and mustache of a black-and-white movie star. He's been in the dog-show world for more than forty years.

The galleries at the breed stage are always small—there's so much going on at once, and a lot of folks wait until the contests later in the day. Right now maybe thirty people are sitting or standing around the edges of the ring. They cheer louder for Laura and Striker than for any other dogs. Laura's wearing a yellow armband with the number nine. Every handler gets an armband with the number their dog has been assigned for the competition. "Armband" is too fancy a word for it—it's just a yellow card held down by a rubber band. Handlers like Laura who show multiple dogs at one show have to keep switching out the cards. Laura also has a long silver comb jammed underneath the rubber band. Every time she and Striker stop moving, she touches up his chest fur.

Gschwender brings in one batch of dogs, inspects each one, then checks the list and brings out another batch. Watching the judging at the breed stage can be baffling, even though Westminster is simpler than most. At regular shows, the competitors in a breed are subdivided into classes by age, gender, and type of handler (owner or hired gun, amateur or professional). Occasionally there are further subdivisions for things like the color of the dog. Sometimes so many dogs are entered in a given breed that there end up being six or seven classes. The judge has to pick a winner of each class. What this means in practice is that a few dogs at a time get shuttled into and out of the ring like butlers in a Broadway farce. Those winners compete against one another for Winners Dog (best male) and Winners Bitch. Then those two dogs move on to the final breed judging, along with any remaining dogs that hold the title of champion. (We'll get to the champion part later. It's complicated.) The judge chooses Best of Breed from that final group. If you're trying to follow along, and you don't know which dogs belong to which classes, God help you. There's no PA announcer to explain.

Westminster judging is more streamlined. Every dog that qualifies is already at the champion level. All the age and handler stuff goes out the window. The only separate classes are dogs and bitches. Besides Best of Breed, at least three other dogs get ribbons: Best of Opposite Sex, plus Select Dog (the second-best male) and Select Bitch (the second-best female). Judges can also hand out Awards of Merit to other dogs based on the size of the field.

The bottom line is, all this takes a while. The rule of thumb for breed judging is two minutes per dog. With twenty-six dogs, it'll take about an hour to whittle down the Samoyeds. For the dogs and their handlers, most of that is waiting. Striker is fantastic at waiting. Most of the other dogs keep looking up at their owners, pleading for scritches or treats. Striker seems to barely notice what's going on. When Laura tells him to be still, he stares off into the distance. His normal stance is an almost perfect stack—the kind of pose it can take a show dog months to learn.

One of the defining traits of the Samoyed is something called the Sammy smile. The theory goes that as the breed evolved in the bitter Siberian winters, the corners of its mouth began to turn upward so its drool wouldn't leak out and freeze. People talk about their dogs smiling all the time, but the Samoyed is one of the only dogs that can actually form a smile, even with its mouth closed. What that means, when Striker is standing still and staring into the distance, is that it looks like he's reliving a fond memory, like a choice piece of steak or an especially pleasurable hump.

He takes quick short breaths that make him look like he's nodding to an EDM beat: *oontz oontz oontz.*

This is a part of show quality, too. Most of the dogs that win dog shows aren't jumpers, at least not in the ring. They have an inner stillness that I tend to associate with people who are either enlightened or empty-headed. Al McGuire, the great college basketball coach, used to say he didn't like really smart players—they were too aware of the crowd and the noise to play with the proper focus. This is not to say Striker isn't smart. It's just to say he would have made a hell of a point guard.

We humans like to believe we have some cosmic connection with those who came before us. Some of us literally see ghosts. Others feel the spirits of the ancestors. For many of us it's a smaller and more subtle thing. I look in the mirror in the morning and see my dad's eyes, the same shade of blue, the same shape at the corners. The longer I spent on the dog-show circuit, the more I started wondering if dogs could somehow sense their own pasts. A pure-bred dog is functionally a human creation. But does it occasionally feel the tingle of the wolf? And what would those wolves think, thirty thousand years ago, if you could somehow travel back in time and show them how it all ended up?

When I first heard the distinction that dog-show people make—show quality vs. pet quality—the main thing I took from it was the subtle dig. As in, there was a category of dog that was only good enough to be a pet. Given my general preference for, well, underdogs, my instinct was to flip the idea. Pet-quality dogs don't have to put up with the shit that show dogs do. Pet dogs get to do what they want most of the day. Pet quality means freedom.

Of course, that argument falls apart under the slightest pressure. John Berger, a British writer and painter, put it this way in his 1980 essay "Why Look at Animals?": "The pet is either sterilised or sexually isolated, extremely limited in its exercise, deprived of almost all other animal contact, and fed with artificial foods. This is the material process which lies behind the truism that pets come to resemble their masters or mistresses. They are creatures of their owner's way of life."

In other words, dogs might be drawn to us because we haven't given them a whole lot of choice.

It's hard to imagine that a dog in charge of its own free will would choose to spend years of its life in a show ring. But dogs probably wouldn't choose to pull sleds or fetch dead ducks, either. We have manufactured a creature so skilled at meeting our needs that it feels like it was their idea all along.

But look at it from the other direction. If you own a dog, there are surely days when you don't feel like getting up and walking it. Nobody enjoys bending down to pick up a mound of dog shit, the warm stench separated from your skin by a thin membrane of grocery bag. What might a dog think of that? *Here comes the person who trails around behind me every morning, picking up any mess I leave behind. So well trained.*

The late children's book author Amy Krouse Rosenthal once said: "Pay attention to what you pay attention to." Humans pay attention to dogs more than any other living creature on Earth. And America pays more attention to dogs than any other country does. Numbers on pet ownership are sketchy—there's no census for pets—but the American Veterinary Medical Association estimated that, as of 2020, there were somewhere between eighty-four million and ninety million dogs in the United States—about one dog for every four people. (Cats are next with somewhere between sixty million and sixty-two million. The numbers drop off fast when you get to fish and birds and such.) Dog owners spend an average of more than $900 a year on their dogs. The single biggest reason first-time homeowners buy a house is to make space for a dog.

But those are measures of quantity. They don't explain quality—not show quality or pet quality but *dog quality*, that mysterious essence we extracted from the wolf and molded over tens of thousands of years until we ended up with not just tools but soulmates.

These days, instead of fire and bones, the warm glow is a television and the food scraps might be nachos. But in some ways we are in the same place as when man was just beginning and dog did not yet exist. Drawn to each other. Learning about each other. Working out the terms of the deal.

Gschwender, the judge, has culled the twenty-six Samoyeds down to ten. He's ready to pick the winner.

The dogs and handlers arrange themselves in a wide oval around him. He strolls around, taking one last look, and then calls one to the middle. He lines up another dog behind it. Then a third, a fourth, a fifth, a *sixth*. He's only required to give out four ribbons. Laura and Striker are still standing with the other dogs. It would be a huge upset if they got completely shut out.

It is possible that the guy who looks like an old film star has a sense of drama.

He walks over to Laura and Striker and waves them to the front of the line.

Laura does a little hop when she gets there. Striker, noticing, does a hop of his own.

They are through to the Working Group round tonight. That

round will be under the TV tent, live on FOX Sports. One step closer to Best in Show. And one step closer to something else, something most of the people watching don't know about.

Westminster is the pinnacle for a show dog, and most of their owners and handlers want them to finish on top. It's common for a show dog to retire after their final Westminster. Striker has run the American circuit three times, on top of his career in Canada. He's six years old, around the time most show dogs start to fade. A Sussex spaniel named Stump won Westminster at age ten, back in 2009, but he was a huge outlier. Nutrition and training can cover up a lot of natural aging. But in the end, time is undefeated.

Striker's owners and Laura first discussed it months ago, and they've held to their agreement.

No matter what happens, this is Striker's last show.

Pee Break

DOG HATERS, RANKED

#5

The Wicked Witch of the West

"I'll get you, my pretty. And your little dog, too!"

#4

Ambrose Bierce

Satirist of the late nineteenth and early twentieth century, author of "A Dissertation on Dogs": "Because, some thousands of years ago, when we wore other skins than our own and sat enthroned upon our haunches, tearing tangles of tendons from raw bones with our teeth, the dog ministered purveyorwise to our savage needs, we go on cherishing him to this day, when his only function is to lie sun-soaken on a door mat and insult us as we pass in and out, enamored of his fat superfluity."

#3

Greg Stillson

Villain in Stephen King's novel *The Dead Zone*. We meet him as a traveling Bible salesman who encounters a snarling dog outside a farmhouse. After making sure no one is home, Stillson sprays tear gas in the dog's eyes and kicks it to death. I have never wanted a bad guy to die so much in my life.

#2

Seinfeld

In season 3's "The Dog," Jerry goes crazy after agreeing to take care of a dog for its ill owner. (Jerry: "I got a wild animal in the house. He's deranged. Maybe he's got rabies. I can get lockjaw." Elaine: "If only.") In season 7's "The Engagement," a different dog drives *Elaine* crazy to the point she, Newman, and Kramer steal it and drop it off miles away—only to get busted when the dog returns with an incriminating scrap of fabric from Kramer's shirt.

#1

Cruella de Vil

Kidnaps puppies! To turn them into fur coats! Disney is *dark*, man.

2

THE FANCY

I am interested in the notion that people can become so obsessed by their world that they lose sense and awareness of how they appear to other people.

—Christopher Guest, director of *Best in Show*

We are a tribeless nation hungry for tribes.

—Wright Thompson, *Pappyland*

They booed the poodle.

This was at Westminster 2020, in Madison Square Garden, just a few weeks before COVID emptied sporting arenas around the country. It was my first Westminster. And from inside the Garden, I noticed something I hadn't known from watching the show on TV: the crowd gets pretty beered up.

The final seven dogs that year included a clear crowd favorite: a golden retriever named Daniel. Golden retrievers have been one of the most popular dogs in America for decades. They originated in Scotland, and you should know for entertainment purposes that the generally recognized founder of the breed was a man named

Dudley Coutts Marjoribanks, who was referred to as Lord Tweed-mouth.

If a crowd can collectively swoon, the Garden crowd swooned over Daniel. He looked like a living honeycomb. His Brad Pitt hair swayed as he loped around the ring. The crowd cheered every time he moved.

The anti-Daniel was a black standard poodle bitch named Siba. She had one of those preposterous poodle haircuts. Poodles, of course, are not born with preposterous haircuts. Those haircuts once had a practical purpose. In Germany, where poodles were created, the dogs were bred by hunters to fetch ducks. They were designed to have thick curls to insulate them from cold water. But they wound up with such dense fur that it was hard for them to swim. So their owners shaved the poodles except for the spots that most needed to stay warm—chest, head, feet. As they came out of the fields and into homes, that fur proved perfect for sculpting. Groomers kept shaving parts of the poodle but went wild with what was left. The poor poodle ended up as a hybrid from hell: duck-hunter chic.

It turns out that duck-hunter chic is the kind of thing that gets a dog laughed at on the street but beloved in the dog-show ring.

Dog shows require poodles' coats to be trimmed into one of two variations: the English Saddle or the Continental Clip. (There's a simpler cut for puppies.) In both styles, groomers shave the face, feet, most of the tail, and most of each leg. The English Saddle leaves a swath of fur around the rear and an extra puff around the hind legs. Siba sported a modified Continental, with a ball of fur in front of the tail. From the rib cage back, she was mostly naked. But the really striking part was her front end. The top of her head was shaped into a massive pompon, and a waterfall of black fur sprouted downward from the vicinity of each ear.

This did not impress the Bud Light drinkers at the Garden. She got mild applause, if any.

Toward the end, the judge, Robert Slay, had the dogs take one more lap around the ring. The fans started chanting for Daniel.

Here is where I remind you that the dogs were not, technically, competing against each other. Officially, Slay was measuring them against their own breed's standard. But at dog shows, I've come to think, they are unofficially measured against something else: what people inside the dog-show world consider to be a great dog, as opposed to what regular human beings consider to be a great dog.

The insider term for the dog-show world is "the fancy." As in, *Are you part of the fancy?*

Daniel was a thousand lovable dog-things. But he was not fancy.

The poodle won.

And the fans booed. Not all of them, but enough to notice.

Backstage, afterward, every dog person I talked to said Siba was the right choice.

Standard poodles have won Best in Show at Westminster five times. A golden has never won.

As Siba and her handler posed for pictures, workers were already sweeping up the debris and collecting the stray cups left under the seats. It felt like a pub closing up for the night. Which made sense, given how Westminster began.

· · ·

Like many things great and terrible, it started with a bunch of white guys having a few drinks.

They hung out at the bar in the Westminster Hotel at Sixteenth Street and Irving Place in Manhattan, a block from Union Square. The hotel is long gone now, but back then, in 1876, it was an upscale place, popular with British tourists. Charles Dickens slept there.

It was eleven years after the end of the Civil War, and a new moment in America was dawning. Historians call it the Second Industrial Revolution. Railroads connected the country. Workers moved from farms into factories. Alexander Graham Bell made the first telephone call. But at the same time, frontier America was still raw and bloody. Native American forces led by Crazy Horse killed George Custer at the Battle of Little Bighorn in what is now Montana. Wild Bill Hickok was shot to death in a poker game in Deadwood, holding aces and eights.

Mark Twain coined the term "The Gilded Age" for that span roughly between the end of the Civil War and the start of the twentieth century. It wasn't a compliment. He was describing the thin film of wealth that disguised massive poverty, especially among the millions of immigrants who flooded the country to chase American dreams. A vast distance existed between those at the top and those at the bottom. At the same time there was a growing middle space where people had a chance to cash in on a piece of the new America. The regulars at the Westminster bar weren't as rich as the robber barons. But they had some of that new money and the urge to spend it. Some of them spent it on dogs.

It does not take long for a hunter to brag on his dogs. Especially after a whiskey or two. Sometime in 1876, maybe even before, the dog men at the bar decided to form a kennel club, at least partly to decide whose dogs were best. They decided to call it the Westminster Breeding Association, after the place where they gathered.

The club founders included a banker, a yachtsman, a wine merchant, and the kennel editor of a publication called *Forest and Stream* (later absorbed by its main rival, *Field and Stream*). Two others were brothers: a doctor named William Seward Webb and a lawyer named H. Walter Webb. They recruited their older half brother, Alexander Stewart Webb, to help organize the group and lead it. He would bring the group immediate respectability and the glow of a Civil War hero.

At Gettysburg, back in July 1863, General Webb had stood at the Union front while the Confederates launched a fusillade as prelude to the desperate blitz that became known as Pickett's Charge. The story goes that as the cannonballs and bullets flew around him, Webb coolly smoked a cigar. When the Confederate troops finally charged, Webb joined the battle and was shot twice, but the Union forces won in a rout. Today there is a bronze statue of Webb at the battlefield, posed so he stares out at the trees, leaning on his sword, his left hand cocked at the hip.

Less than a year later, at the Battle of Spotsylvania Court House, Webb was shot again—this time a bullet went in the corner of his right eye socket and came out his right ear. The *New York Times* published a notice of his death. Not only was he not dead, but the bullet didn't seem to slow him down that much. After healing he returned to the army until the war ended, then served as an instructor at West Point. In 1869 he became president of the City College of New York and held that job for thirty-three years.

Webb had a pointer named Fritz, but he doesn't seem to have

been a dog lover on the level of the men at the Westminster bar. But someone who ran a university and had commanded troops could damn well put on a dog show. The main issue was, it wasn't quite clear yet exactly what a dog show should be.

People had been gathering their dogs for public displays long before there was anything like an official dog show. There's evidence of an exhibition of Schipperkes* held in Brussels around 1690.

In the 1700s, there are several records of foxhound exhibitions. In 1834, a man named Charlie Aistrop showed off several breeds at his pub in London. It was an odd turn because Aistrop had once run the Westminster Pit, a notorious dive that held dogfights, cockfights, and even bear fights. The bear fights ended when one of them killed Aistrop's wife while she tried to feed it.

Social clubs, civic groups, and county fairs brought together dogs for various events throughout the early 1800s. They were more celebration than competition. The first event most historians link to modern dog shows happened in Newcastle, England, in 1859. A poultry show was the main event, and the dogs were a side attraction. There were sixty dogs, all males and all hunting dogs—pointers or setters. The difference between this show and earlier ones was that the organizers arranged for judges and gave out awards. The big prizes were two double-barreled shotguns. The surprise for the organizers was the size of the crowd—some fifteen thousand people, far more than expected.

*Schipperke, pronounced *SHEEP-er-ker*, Americanized as *SKIP-er-kee*: Wedge-shaped black Belgian dog, ten to fifteen pounds, bred to kill rats on barges, nicknamed "little captain" or sometimes "little black devil."

That led the same organizers to hold another show in Birmingham, England, in 1860, adding more breeds and a separate category for puppies. That show was even more successful. Dog lovers across Europe copied the idea. Some Americans had surely heard about dog shows by then—either through sporting journals or through the trade of purebred dogs to and from the States. But instead of dog shows we had the war, and the years of recovery that followed.

The first American dog show, by most accounts, was in Chicago in 1874. Like the show in Newcastle, it was limited to pointers and setters—twenty-one in all. There were no particular rules for dog shows at the time, so the judges just wrote critiques of each dog. A setter named Grouse got this review: "Very fat, great depth of chest, fine head."

Four months later, a former Confederate soldier named P. H. Bryson held a show in Memphis. The story goes that Bryson came home from the war wounded and nearly dead, but hunting with a bird dog helped ease him back to health. He and his brother started acquiring dogs and ended up building a kennel for setters. Bryson wrote pieces for a magazine called *Turf, Field and Farm*, urging Americans to hold dog shows. That's where the organizers of the show in Chicago got the idea. The Memphis event made an evolutionary step by becoming the first to name a Best in Show. It was also the first to have some controversy about the Best in Show. (More about that in a few chapters, when we go deeper into judging.)

News of these shows filtered to the Westminster men, and they were eager to get involved. They helped a group of Philadelphia dog lovers stage a show there in 1876 as part of an exposition celebrating America's centennial. That event also drew big crowds.

In early 1877, the Westminster Breeding Association decided it was time to hold a show in New York. Dog shows were clearly popular but also an idea not fully formed, with no real rules, no governing body, nothing in particular to make them special.

The guys from the Westminster bar wanted to change all that. They wanted something grand. So they reached out to the grandest new place in New York.

You know P. T. Barnum. Founder of what eventually became the Ringling Bros. and Barnum & Bailey Circus. Huckster and hoaxster extraordinaire. Profiteer from Siamese twins and bearded ladies and others he exploited. Credited with saying, "There's a sucker born every minute." (Chances are he never said it, though he definitely believed it.) Barnum also dabbled in dogs. He put on exhibitions in the early 1860s at his American Museum and did one in Boston in 1863 that he called the Great National Dog Show. He gave out huge prizes; the winners often got $1,000—the equivalent of $25,000 today. But these shows weren't about pedigrees. "SINGING DOGS, LAUGHING DOGS, CRYING DOGS, DANCING DOGS, PERFORMING DOGS . . . ," said one of his posters, which also advertised a Siberian bloodhound "whose GIANT proportions are more like a horse than a dog."

In 1874, Barnum built a ten-thousand-seat open arena for his circus at East Twenty-Sixth Street and Madison Avenue, on the site of an old railyard. The building was 420 feet long and the walls 28 feet high. A canvas tent covered the whole thing when it rained. He called the arena the Great Roman Hippodrome, or sometimes Barnum's Monster Classical and Geological Hippodrome. One of his early ads touted a "GRAND MENAGERIE of 500 rare Wild Beasts . . . Roman Chariot Racing, Hurdle and Flat Races, Elephant, Camel, Pony and Monkey Racing."

But after just two years, Barnum got tired of New York weather and decided a traveling circus was a better idea. He leased the building to Patrick Gilmore, a bandleader best known for writing the lyrics to "When Johnny Comes Marching Home." Gilmore decorated the arena with plants and renamed it Gilmore's Garden. He started holding concerts there and also rented out the building for flower shows, beauty contests, and revivals. Barnum's circus ran there when it came back through town.

The Westminster Breeding Association—which, somewhere along the way, changed its name to the Westminster Kennel Club—rented Gilmore's Garden for May 8–10, 1877, for $1,500. They billed the show as the First Annual New York Bench Show of Dogs. A bench show means that dogs are kept out in the open, on partitioned benches, when they're not competing. That way, fans can come look at the dogs up close or even pet them. It was one of the many parts of a dog show that organizers were still figuring out. It was a tradition Westminster would keep.

The kennel club had put the word out through newspapers and sporting magazines and among the informal network of dog breeders. *Forest and Stream* noted that the club would award prizes including gold coins—although it noted that if any gentleman was opposed to competing for money, he could have the coin melted down into a medal.

Entries flooded in from all over the US and Europe. Remember, just three years before, the first official American dog show featured twenty-one dogs. Westminster's inaugural show had somewhere around *nine hundred*. Many dogs were entered in more than one category, so the total number of entries was more like twelve hundred.

New York turned out. The first day there were eight thousand spectators. Each of the next two days brought more than twenty thousand. They added an extra day to the show. They made so much money that the kennel club donated the last day's profits—nearly $2,000—to the American Society for the Prevention of Cruelty to Animals. An ASPCA official tried to give a speech at the dog show, but he was drowned out by hundreds of barking dogs. Nobody had trained show dogs to hush.

The judges included the Reverend J. Cumming Macdona, a world-renowned dog authority brought in from Cheshire, England. Uniformed officials walked the dogs into the show ring. Tiffany made silver cups for the winners. Those little details gave the show a veneer of status and wealth. This wasn't P. T. Barnum, with his sideshow oddities and camel races. This was an event meant for the society page. It was intended to elevate not just dogs, but dog people.

The members of Westminster brought their own dogs to the show, but dogs that were part of the official kennel club weren't eligible for competition. One way to see that is they were avoiding a conflict of interest. Another way is they were creating a higher tier—a group above such things as silver cups and ribbons.

There was no award for Best in Show.

That December, the Westminster men met to incorporate their kennel club and plan the next year's show. This one would have a simpler title: the Westminster Dog Show. They had proved that a dog show could be a big deal in America. And they had tapped into something else that was just becoming clear: having a dog as a pet was becoming a symbol of upward mobility. It was one thing to own a dog that worked for you. It was another to own a dog that didn't have to.

In some ways, this is Queen Victoria's fault. Or to her credit.

She reigned over the British Empire for sixty-three years, from 1837 to her death in 1901. And Lord, did the queen love her animals.

At various points in her life, she had Shetland ponies, a herd of goats, a donkey, and a parrot named Coco. But her real passion was dogs. Everyone in England knew of her childhood dog Dash, a Cavalier King Charles spaniel*; Islay, her Skye terrier†; and Noble, her favorite collie.

There's a famous painting from 1843 called *Windsor Castle in Modern Times*, painted by Sir Edwin Landseer. It depicts Prince Albert just home from the hunt—a few dead gamebirds are scattered on the floor—while Victoria and their daughter welcome him home. Four of the family dogs romp around the scene, one of them on its hind legs, begging. The formal garden outside and the lush furnishings reveal the riches behind the scene. But if you focus on the people and the dogs, it could be an ordinary day in

---

*Cavalier King Charles spaniel: Named for two King Charleses, father and son, in seventeenth-century England—the king's supporters were called Cavaliers. Around fifteen pounds. Four distinct color patterns. Urban legend holds that they have free passage into any building in the UK, according to a king's decree.
†Skye terrier: Shaggy, low-slung dog that looks like it ate a Slinky. The story goes that after Mary, Queen of Scots, was beheaded in 1587, her Skye was found under her petticoat.

an ordinary house. No commoner could afford Victoria's jewels or her gowns or her shoes. They couldn't live in one of her castles. But they could have the same kind of dog.

For thousands of years after dogs and people bonded, no one but the wealthy kept a dog as a pet. Virtually every dog breed we know today was created to do some kind of work. But in the nineteenth century, as the industrializing world created a middle class—first in England, a little later in the US—a pet became a symbol of freedom, money, and leisure. For a while the preferred pet was a songbird in a cage. Then maybe a goldfish in a bowl. But eventually, dogs began to dominate.

Early dog shows favored dogs that still did hard labor, like the hunting breeds owned by the men who started Westminster. But by the time of their first dog show, the entries already included half a dozen categories of terrier, including twenty-one dogs described as "Toy Terriers, Not Exceeding 5 Lbs." Most terriers started out as working dogs, and maybe some of the Westminster terriers were still out catching groundhogs and whatnot, but by the late 1800s, families in cities were starting to keep them around the house.

That closer physical connection brought a closer emotional connection. In earlier days, farmers didn't think much about drowning a sack of kittens or shooting a dog that had passed its prime. But that was when a cat or a dog was worth less, financially and otherwise, than a cow or a pig. Much in the same way that dogs crept from the edge of the fire into the center of early human life, they crept from the pack of household beasts into the inner circle. And as they did, they checked a box for those households on the way up the ladder of status. To own a dog meant you could afford a dog, that you had room for a dog, that you had time for a dog. Those were the little luxuries of the middle class.

Dog shows were one of the places where all the classes touched. J. P. Morgan, maybe the most powerful banker in American history, got hooked on collies after seeing them at Westminster in 1888. He spent a million dollars to build a kennel at his estate in Highland Falls, New York, and imported a kennel master from England to run it. He bought whole lines of British collies. He started entering the dogs at Westminster in 1893, and they soon dominated the breed; a *New York Times* clip about the 1899 show lists Morgan's dogs winning all nine collie categories. But none of his dogs were ever considered *the* best, and in England there were rumors that breeders had fleeced Morgan by selling him substandard dogs. Morgan eventually got out of the dog-show business, but he kept a few collies as pets. His favorite, Sefton Hero, supposedly slept under his bed. Rich people: they're just like us.

The thing is, at a dog show like Westminster, people could see J. P. Morgan's dogs—even pet them—for the price of a ticket. And people in the new middle class could spend a little money— way less than Morgan did—to show their dogs in the same ring. Regular folks could imagine common ground between themselves and the upperest of the upper crust. *They love dogs. I love dogs. Maybe we're not so far apart.*

As the wealthy reached down, the less wealthy reached up. Those early dog shows were filled with spectators in their finest clothes. (People also dressed up for ball games, another place that flattened out class divides.) The world is much more casual now. Westminster hangs on to some of the old ways—the Best in Show judge wears a tux or an evening gown—but most fans show up in jeans. There is one time when the fancy really is still fancy, when you can get a glimpse of how dog shows first caught hold.

But it only happens every five years. Sometimes every six.

I got out of my Honda Accord and walked into the 1920s.

Women shimmied in flapper dresses. Men wore bowler hats and vests with pocket watches. They strolled across the green of a county park like Civil War reenactors, but what they were reenacting was the Morris & Essex Kennel Club show, a century-old event once hosted by one of the richest couples in American history.

In 1907, Geraldine Rockefeller—one of *the* Rockefellers, daughter of a cofounder of Standard Oil—married Marcellus Hartley Dodge, who had inherited $60 million from his financier grandfather and eventually became chairman of Remington Arms, the gun and ammo maker. As rich as Dodge was, he was no Rockefeller: she brought an estimated $100 million to the marriage. Dodge already had an estate called Hartley Farms in Harding Township, New Jersey. The couple bought a nearby swath of land and built another estate called Giralda Farms. Eventually, they decided to live separately—he at the old estate and she at the new one. It turned out her real passion was dogs.

Geraldine had a kennel built at Giralda Farms that housed up to 150 dogs at a time, especially her favorites: cocker spaniels and German shepherds. In 1927 she formed the Morris & Essex Kennel Club, naming it after the two counties where the club members lived. That year they held the first Morris & Essex Dog Show on the polo fields at Hartley Farms.

From the beginning it was intended to be a more elegant event than a regular dog show. The night before, there was a dance with a live orchestra. The day of the show, a bell rang at noon and everyone stopped for lunch—served on china for the VIPs and in boxes for everybody else, but all on Mrs. Dodge's dime.

That first year there were 595 dogs entered. But as word spread about the show, the numbers bulged every year. By 1939, the show had a massive total of 4,456 dogs—all judged on the same day in fifty-seven rings. It still ranks as one of the largest dog shows in American history.

The show paused for World War II and then kept going until 1957, when Geraldine Dodge quit putting on the show. It's not clear what happened—some accounts say there was a scheduling conflict with the American Kennel Club; others say she had run out of energy at age seventy-five. She died in 1973 and the show died with her. But she had founded an animal shelter called St. Hubert's that remained on her property. Wayne Ferguson, a Saint Bernard breeder and owner of a pet supply company called Cherrybrook, ended up on the board of St. Hubert's in the 1990s. And one year, a shelter employee mentioned that a bunch of old Morris & Essex artifacts were stashed in the attic. Ferguson took a look and got the idea to bring back the show—and to bring back the feel of that time along with it.

They started again in 2000 with plans to hold the show every five years. That worked until COVID canceled the show in 2020. So they postponed it until 2021, which was when I arrived at Colonial Park in Somerset, New Jersey, to walk into the past.

It worked, sort of. But if you let your focus slide, 2021 came back into view. Some of the fans brought camp chairs and Crocs.

Golf carts shuttled judges from the parking lots. A merch table sold Brewscuits ("beer grain biscuits for dogs"). Not everybody dressed up. But the ones who did absolutely went for it. My favorite was a guy who wore a red suit, a matching fedora, red-and-white oxford shoes, and black-and-white checked socks. If you had told me he was a villain in the new Batman movie, I would've bought it.

Morris & Essex was when I first really noticed Laura King and Striker. I'd been tracking them in the weekly show-dog rankings in *The Canine Chronicle* magazine; at the moment, Striker had the number one overall ranking. He won his breed and the Working Group at Morris & Essex and made the final seven. A uniformed bugler came out and played what I always think of as the Kentucky Derby trumpet blast (it's a military tune titled "First Call"). By then it was dark, and the show had been going on for more than twelve hours. So there wasn't exactly a surge of energy. The crowd had dwindled to the dog diehards. But Laura and Striker looked gorgeous there under the floodlights, she in a black sequined dress, he in his normal attire. When they trotted around the ring, you could hear a movie score swelling in the background. Even among the very best dogs and handlers in the world, they looked special. At least to me.

They did not win Morris & Essex. Best in Show went to a Pekingese named Wasabi—the same dog that beat Striker in the final round at Westminster 2021 just a few months before. I had been paying attention to Wasabi and a couple of other dogs as ones to follow around for a while leading up to Westminster '22. After that Best in Show at Morris & Essex, I decided to spend more time on Striker. It wasn't because I thought he might contend—by then, that was obvious. It was something else. A weird little spark in my brain. Something to do with that "Sammy smile" and the moment and the setting and the Morris & Essex vibe. And something else I had been thinking about that pulled me back even further in time.

I have a list of weird questions I plan on asking whatever being is in charge of the afterlife. One of them is this: When was the first time somebody smiled in a photo? One of the most fascinating things about early photography is that nobody smiled. There's no conclusive answer as to why, but there are several theories. A photo took a long time to expose back then, and it was hard to hold a smile that long. Folks were more likely to have bad teeth, so they smiled less in general. Sitting for a portrait was a rare and momentous thing, meant to be taken seriously.

Those all make sense. But there's an exception: when you look at old photos of people *with their dogs*, the people tend to be smiling. That holds all the way back to the late 1800s, when both family dogs and family photos were new to the middle class. There's a photo I keep on my computer desktop, something I found one day while scrolling through old dog photos online. Somebody saved it on a Pinterest page. It's a young woman in a modest dress with a bit of frill at the neck. Her hair is held back by a ribbon. She's leaning against a dog—an Australian shepherd, I think, or something close to it. Her left arm is wrapped around him and her right hand is on his chest, and they are cheek to cheek, both looking at the camera. The smile on her face is quiet but content. She looks blissful with her place in the world.

Those years when dog shows were dawning were years when

people strived for property and status and money and pleasure. Dogs could symbolize any or all of those things. But they also could bring a simple sense of joy. If you had a dog, even if you had to sit there half the day to get your picture taken, it was hard to keep from smiling.

CARTOON DOGS, RANKED

#5

Goofy

Fully clothed, even though Mickey wears pants and no shirt, Donald wears a shirt and no pants, and Pluto wears nothing but a collar. The question from *Stand by Me* remains: What the hell is Goofy? Overdressed, at the very least.

#4

Tramp

Costar of the first rom-com for kids. Enthusiastic believer in interbreed relationships. Lover, not a fighter, but will kill a rat if he has to. Likes Italian food.

#3
Hong Kong Phooey

Secret identity of police janitor Penrod "Penry" Pooch. Bills himself as kung fu master but is terrible at kung fu. Voiced by the great Scatman Crothers. On almost no one's list of greatest cartoons. This is *my* list, dammit.

#2
Scooby-Doo

Perpetually underrated crime solver (similar to Lt. Columbo). Early adopter of #vanlife. Obviously high. Everything would have been fine if it hadn't been for you meddling kids.

#1
Snoopy

The king. Decorated fighter pilot. Slick-fielding shortstop. Root beer connoisseur. Early proponent of Riverdance. According to Charlie Brown, spelled B-E-A-G-E-L.

3

RIDING BETTY WHITE

They call it a cluster. It's not officially short for "clusterfuck." But the "fuck" is sometimes implied.

A cluster is a typical weekend on the dog-show circuit. If Westminster is the Super Bowl, clusters are the regular season. It's where dogs earn the points they need to qualify for Westminster. A dog can't get to the big show unless it shines in the little ones, in the anonymous civic centers and livestock arenas, with almost nobody watching. That's where the top dogs emerge, the pretenders wilt, and the handlers crash after eighteen-hour days. It is a whirlwind of fur and chaos.

At one show, I watched a pro handler from Georgia named Justin Smithey shuffle whippets* in and out of the show ring like a juggler keeping seven balls in the air. He had gotten up before

---

*Whippet: Cut-down version of the greyhound. Bred as a rabbit hunter but beloved by Victorian England gamblers as a racing dog. Top speed of 35 mph. If you came to this footnote to find out about huffing nitrous oxide, boy are you in the wrong book.

dawn to deliver a dog to a client at the Atlanta airport. Then he and his wife, Cheslie, had driven to McDonald, Tennessee, where they were both showing dogs at the weekend shows there. (Two of the days were devoted to the North Georgia Kennel Club, which meant the North Georgia Kennel Club show was in Tennessee. Just roll with it.) Somewhere along the way they had picked up a dog fancier who had flown over from South Korea to talk with the Smitheys about some dog breeding possibilities. The Korean guy ended up as an unofficial assistant, holding on to half a dozen whippets at once like a New York dog walker. Whenever Smithey had a few seconds in between, he pulled out his phone to watch the live feed of a *horse* show that one of his horses was entered in. That's when I started to feel the full weight of the word "cluster."

It's called a cluster because several kennel clubs pool their resources to have a group of shows in the same place. Think of the golf tour, inverted: a golf weekend is a single four-day tournament, but a typical dog-show cluster is four single-day events. The American Kennel Club sanctions about 1,500 official shows a year. Most weeks there are half a dozen clusters scattered across America. That means hundreds of dog handlers, and thousands of dogs, spend every week crisscrossing the country. The first thing you see when you get to a dog show is a parking lot full of Winnebagos and pop-up campers and sprinter vans. Outside most of them you'll find exercise pens (the insider term is "expen" or "X-pen")—portable wire enclosures where dogs can hang out while they wait for showtime. The lots are a funky cologne of exhaust fumes and dog pee and cedar chips.

If you didn't know what you were walking into, you just had to look at the bumper stickers.

DOGS 2020, BECAUSE PEOPLE SUCK

**LORD, HELP ME TO BE
THE PERSON MY DOG THINKS I AM**

HONK TO SEE MY WEINER

I came to think of the whole scene as something like the eternal caravan of Deadheads, except fueled by boxed wine and Big Macs instead of LSD and falafel.

Just like a Dead concert, everyone experiences a dog show a little differently. To me, especially at first, it felt fast and slow at the same time. The judging in an individual round goes so quick that it can take a minute to figure out who won. But the full show itself is a commitment; if you arrive for the national anthem and stick around for Best in Show, you might not see the sun all day.

From the inside, a dog show plays out as a series of micro-dramas, not just in the show rings but around them, involving the dogs but mostly the humans. Peggy Sprawn, a dog handler I met along the way, called it "our little circus." But a circus has just three rings. A dog show has six or eight or twelve, sometimes all going at once. And everybody's mixed in together, from the greenest amateur handlers to an in-demand pro like Striker's handler, Laura King.

Laura and her partner, Robin Novack, sometimes have eighteen or twenty dogs going on the same day. They basically need to be in three places at once, four times a week, fifty weeks out of the year.

Which is why it made sense when I climbed the stairs of their RV and saw the sign on the far wall:

WELCOME

TO THE

SHITSHOW

They call the RV Betty White. Partly because it's white. Partly because Betty White was funny as hell. Mostly because Betty White spent much of her life advocating for animal causes, from the Los Angeles Zoo to American Humane (the group that monitors animal treatment on movie sets). You can find pictures of her hugging lions and bears and parrots and snakes. But dogs were her favorite. At one point she had twenty-six.

The RV that Laura and Robin named for her is a custom-built United Specialties motor home, a forty-two-footer. The back sixteen feet has been transformed into a portable kennel with dual AC units and twenty dog crates bolted to one wall. The front cabin is often crawling with smaller dogs racing underfoot and generally whipping up chaos. Towels and combs are flung everywhere. It's a college dorm room that smells like dog shampoo. I didn't want to leave, and couldn't for a while once two spaniels jumped in my lap.

"This is the office," Robin said, throwing up her hands in the universal *Whaddaya gonna do?* gesture.

Laura and Robin technically live on a five-acre spread in the

Illinois countryside just south of the Quad Cities, where the Mississippi River divides Illinois from Iowa. Their home is attached to their business, Daybreak Kennel, which has indoor/outdoor kennel space and grooming stations and dog runs and a big tree to pee on.

But for most of the year their real home is Betty White. They typically leave Daybreak on Tuesday or Wednesday to drive to that weekend's cluster. Unless they bomb out early, they're almost always showing until late on Sunday. Then they drive home overnight. They stay for a day or two, long enough to swap out dogs and stock up on supplies. Then the cycle repeats. Their days last from dawn to midnight, sometimes longer. Once, when I was talking to Laura at a show, a couple of her clients texted her at noon to say they were heading to breakfast. "'We're just going for breakfast,'" she said, reading the text and laughing. "God, I love these people. Are you fucking kidding me?"

At the shows, most of the dogs sleep in the RV, along with one or two assistants Robin and Laura bring along for the trip. Robin and Laura sleep in a hotel, with a few select dogs—the frail ones and the champs. Striker earned his spot on the floor at the Residence Inn.

(A quick story. When dog-show folks stay at hotels, they often mark off their parking spots with traffic cones so they can come and go without having to find a new spot for their motor home every time. At Westminster one year, an RV had parked in the spot right outside my room. A couple of days into the show, I got back and saw the spot had been cleared. I figured they had gone home, so I parked there. The next morning I came out to a furious handwritten note on my windshield from a woman named Linda, who accused me of stealing her traffic cones. "GOD SEES YOU!" she wrote at the end. Linda, if you happen to be reading this, it wasn't me. But based on your note, I'm not broken up that it happened.)

All this is absolute luxury compared with how Laura started. When she and her mother drove to dog shows in the early '80s, they took a camper that was so outdated it had an icebox instead of a refrigerator. "A sandwich for lunch and a sandwich for dinner," she said. "Showering in all of the finest fairgrounds in the country."

Laura's mother got the family involved in show dogs. She had owned a couple of German shepherds that had hip problems. At one vet visit somebody asked if her dog was a Belgian sheepdog—similar to a German shepherd, but smaller and with a longer coat. Laura's mom decided a Belgian sheepdog might be healthier. She bought a puppy, but the seller required that the dog be "finished," or earn champion status as a show dog. So she started out on the dog-show circuit. She named the dog Dora. Laura came along not long after the dog did. She learned to walk by holding on to Dora's tail.

Walk into the weeds with me for a bit while I explain why all these dogs are galivanting from show to show in the first place.

The basic goal for a show dog is to earn the title of champion. A champion dog not only qualifies for shows like Westminster, but earns a title that makes it valuable for breeding. To become a champion, a dog has to earn championship points.

The scoring system is convoluted beyond belief. At AKC-sponsored shows, the number of points a dog can earn depends on the region where the show is being held, the number of dogs and bitches entered in a particular breed, and how many dogs in the breed competition are already champions.

A dog can win one to five championship points at a dog show, depending on the variables. A win of three points or more counts as a major. When a dog gets to fifteen points, it's a champion—as long as it has won two or more majors and has scored points from at least three different judges.

Got all that? Good. Now let's tackle something simpler, like the US tax code.

Theoretically, a dog can earn enough points for a championship in just three shows. As a practical matter, it often takes months or years. Some dogs never get there. So week after week, at all these shows all over the country, dogs that used to chase rabbits and squirrels are now chasing points. And once a dog earns enough points to be officially "finished," its owners can put a CH, for champion, in front of its name.

For many dogs, being finished really is the finish line. They move to other events—like agility competions or field trials. Or they become breeding stock. Or they go back to being full-time pets.

More ambitious handlers and owners have other goals. One reason they enter dogs at so many shows is to accumulate "dogs defeated" points, which are a big-picture look at how well a dog is doing that year. For example, if a dog wins Best in Show at a show with 1,000 entries, it gets 999 points because it beat out 999 other dogs. *Canine Chronicle* keeps a running list of the top dogs in each breed and group for the calendar year, as well as the top one hundred overall. People in the fancy follow those charts like music obsessives used to follow the *American Top 40*.

Westminster keeps its own tally that runs from October through September. That tally matters because it's how Westminster chooses the dogs to invite to the following year's show. They send out invitations to the top five dogs in each breed, plus any other champion dogs that won Best of Breed at a national specialty show (a show devoted to a single breed).

With around two hundred AKC-recognized breeds, those invitations add up to about 1,200 dogs (the normal cap for a Westminster field is 2,500). Owners of other champion dogs can then apply to fill the rest of the slots. It's not guaranteed—if there are more applications than slots, there's a lottery. The winners get mailed their notice in a bright-yellow Westminster envelope that makes an excellent Instagram visual.

The owners of truly special dogs, like Striker, don't have to sweat the lottery. He's been a top dog for years. His people don't worry about just making it to Westminster. They want to win.

But everybody on the dog-show circuit is chasing something. Maybe trophies and ribbons and championships. Maybe invitations to the big show. But there are also quieter quests, things that are more internal, things that can't be measured in points.

"We're very passionate about our dogs," a handler named Michelle Parris tells me as she wipes the tears away.

I had met Michelle in person for the first time about fifteen minutes before. A mutual friend had connected us, and we had agreed to get together at the Victory Lane Classic in Concord, North Carolina, close to my home in Charlotte and Michelle's in Davidson. ("Victory Lane Classic" because this is NASCAR country.) The three-day cluster was held at the Cabarrus Arena and Events Center, one of those multipurpose concrete barns that can host anything from a high school graduation to the Harlem Globetrotters. It checks the key boxes for the dog-show circuit: close to the interstate; cheap parking and lots of it. It ended up drawing about 1,500 dogs a day—on the high end for the regular season. A good place to win points.

One of the quirks of the dog-show world is that amateurs and pros compete against one another. A professional handler might show a dozen or more dogs at a show—some that they work with every week, others they work with occasionally, still others that might be a one-shot deal for a local dog owner. Beyond that are also owner-handlers who just work with their own dogs, and they have levels of their own—some travel the circuit, some do it mostly for fun. Michelle Parris, when I met her, had done some of both. She was in the midst of sorting that out. She was in the midst of sorting out a lot of things.

Michelle sold real estate for a living, but her passion was breeding and showing Italian greyhounds, known among the fancy as IGs, or iggies. If a standard greyhound is a Dodge Charger, and a whippet is a Mustang, an iggie is a Mini Cooper. Regular greyhounds run sixty to seventy pounds, but a normal iggie weighs around ten. (Aristocrats in the Renaissance bred bonsai versions of big dogs for pets.) Michelle loves iggies' delicacy, their playfulness, the gorgeous S curves of their hind legs and back and belly. She showed them frequently—even got one of her dogs to Westminster—until 2019, when her life started slowly falling apart.

It started when she and her longtime partner, Mike Gunkel, broke up. They had met at a Renaissance fair and were together for twelve years. They parted on good terms. Mike kept one of the iggies Michelle had bred. Even after the breakup, he backed her dog-show dreams, emotionally and financially. But she decided to step away from the ring for a while.

When she was finally ready to go back, in early 2020, COVID hit, and dog shows were canceled all over the country.

That July, she got shingles.

That September, Mike died of heart failure.

In the midst of that, the dogs had all sorts of issues. Two of the males got into a fight, and Michelle tore a bicep separating them. One of her dogs got sick. Then another. She took them both to a vet in West Virginia—a guy known in the fancy as a specialist for IGs. One dog healed. The other, called Sky Guy, had an autoimmune disease. There wasn't anything the vet could do. Michelle fed the dog one last vanilla Frosty and said goodbye. IGs usually live fourteen or fifteen years. Sky Guy was not quite six.

Michelle was broken. She had panic attacks. Friends came to help take care of the dogs she had left.

Eventually, the dogs helped bring her back.

Owning a dog forced her into a routine. She couldn't just sleep all day. She had to walk the dogs and feed them. She took care of them and they took care of her.

When I saw her, she had just started going back to dog shows. Not to show, just yet, but to watch. But she was planning to try Westminster that year with a bitch named Clipsey, who had been finished as a champion before the storms blew through Michelle's life. They had been out exercising together. Did a photo shoot for the IG specialty magazine. Fell back into the rhythm of a show dog and a handler. That rhythm comforted her.

She told me the whole story as dogs and handlers raced around us in all directions. It was like being at a busy airport, but one where everybody somehow had a dog. I had been to a bunch of dog shows by then, but it still felt like sensory overload. Michelle barely noticed, except to point out an especially beautiful dog. Even as she cried, she seemed relaxed.

In the chaos of a dog show, she felt her old life coming back.

Now that I've told you her story, I have to tell you something that happened as she was telling it. We were sitting in the lobby of the arena, away from the rings. All of a sudden, from behind me, I heard a woman's stern voice: "No!" Then again, but closer.

I turned to see the woman dragging an absolute unit of a New-foundland* out of the show area and through the lobby. New-foundlands can weigh 150 pounds, and this dog was every bit of it. Soon it was clear why they were having their tug of war. The dog stopped and his back feet started dancing. The universal signal that he was about to take a squat.

"NO!" the handler said, and hauled him toward the back door.

---

*Newfoundlands: Exhibit A of the maxim that the biggest dogs are the sweetest. Bred to help fishermen pull in nets. Partially webbed feet. Legendary for water rescues. The story goes that a Newfoundland rescued Napoleon when he fell off the ship he was using to escape exile in Elba.

This went on for a good fifty or sixty feet, and the dog stopped three or four times along the way, but the handler never gave him a chance to fully assume the position. Finally she got him out the door and onto the concrete plaza outside. She let the lead go slack. He let go a dump the size of a volleyball.

At every dog show there's a cleanup crew that goes around mopping up pee and scooping up poop. The only scoop big enough to handle *that* would have been attached to a front-end loader.

So I was feeling sorry for the cleanup guy who was about to have his day absolutely ruined, while at the same time I was internally laughing my ass off, while at the same time I was feeling the pain and turmoil Michelle was describing.

What I'm saying is, a dog show can put you through some things.

Those emotional swings, and the pageant of the dog show itself, make the fancy ripe to be made fun of.

Best in Show took the deepest dive, building a feature-length mockumentary around a Westminster-ish event called the Mayflower Dog Show. Director Christopher Guest, who also plays owner / handler / aspiring ventriloquist Harlan Pepper, said he got the idea for the movie when he was walking his mutt one day and ran across a woman walking a purebred. She seemed offended that his dog didn't have a pedigree. "What I eventually found out in doing quite a bit of research," he said in an interview with the Ringer, "was that every person who was an owner or handler of a specific breed had a very narrow view of this world, and that any other dog was essentially not worth being alive."

Best in Show, like Guest's other movies, is mostly improvised—he wrote the outline of the movie and let the actors fill in the blanks. We rewatched it a couple of years ago with my wife's mom, and we'd forgotten that it starts with a sex joke: A husband-and-wife handling team worry that their Weimaraner, Beatrice, is depressed because she saw them trying out a new position they found in the Kama Sutra. It's called the Congress of the Cow. Which, as they describe it, sounds a lot like doggy style.

Guest originally wanted to film at an actual dog show, but that didn't work out, so they created one from scratch. They hired dog-show experts to teach the cast members the basics and brought in real show dogs for most of the dog parts. (Winky, the Norwich terrier who wins Best in Show, had the real-life registered name of CAN CH Urchin's Bryllo. The CAN is for Canadian. Its movie name was way better: CH Thank You Neil Sedaka.)

For many fans, the most memorable character is Buck Laughlin, played by Fred Willard, who nails the role of "dog-show announcer who knows nothing about dog shows." Buck is as dumb as a sack of hammers, which makes him hilarious:

"He went for her like she's made out of ham."

"And to think in some countries those dogs are eaten."

"I went to one of those obedience places once . . . it was all going well until they spilled hot candle wax on my private parts."

He's a perfect foil for Trevor Beckwith, played by Jim Piddock, who has the role of "dog show announcer who *does* know about dog shows":

TREVOR: He's being very deliberate. He's known as a deliberate judge.

BUCK: Is that right?

TREVOR: Yes, and an interesting side note, as a matter of fact, he trained to be a priest one time and was in a seminary. Never went through with it all, but it's unusual.

BUCK: Be interesting to find out what went wrong there, but that's a whole other show.

The main person who got upset at *Best in Show* was Joe Garagiola, the former St. Louis Cardinals catcher who became a long-time baseball broadcaster. Garagiola was one of the announcers for Westminster from 1994 to 2002 and was clearly a role model for Buck Laughlin. In a CNN interview after the movie came out, Garagiola said: "I think Fred was playing me. I think he used some lines I wouldn't use, but he's a funny guy and, hey, we all have our tastes. I didn't particularly like the show. I thought the satire went over the top."

In the same interview, he also said: "Different things intrigue me: why a guy would buy a $900 suit and put four pounds of calf liver in his pocket to feed the dog."

Buck Laughlin would have been proud.

People I talked to in Dogland seem ambivalent about *Best in Show*. Some folks were pleased that the filmmakers cared enough to get some of the details right. Other folks rolled their eyes at the handler played by Eugene Levy, who comes off the bench to lead Winky to victory despite having, literally, two left feet. But the movie came out more than twenty years ago. Many of the people working in dog shows now weren't around when it came out. And some of the older folks in the fancy remember a much more ruthless mocking.

In 1997, Conan O'Brien's late-night talk show introduced a character called Triumph the Insult Comic Dog. Triumph was a hand puppet controlled by comedian Robert Smigel, who gave the dog an Eastern European accent and a comic style that might be described as "sleazy sex-obsessed Don Rickles." Triumph first appeared in a studio sketch as the final act in a fake dog show that included dogs doing magic tricks and playing "Dueling Banjos." The writers even gave Triumph a show name (CH Triumph's Honor of Whitehall), which somehow made it funnier when he said Conan had "a great show . . . for me to poop on." That ". . . for me to poop on" would become Triumph's catchphrase. If you ever heard somebody say that in the late '90s and were completely baffled, now you know.

Two years later, Conan sent Triumph to Westminster itself, and he pooped on everything. "Every slutty animal that ever humped its way to the top is represented at Westminster," he said from a perch in the Madison Square Garden stands. "It's not about talent here at Westminster. It's all who you hump." From his spot in the crowd, he shouted: "You suck, German shepherd!" Backstage, where the dogs were benched, he sniffed the butt of a sheepdog and proclaimed: "Lovely bouquet." Then he proceeded to "hump" a series of show dogs while spectators watched in a mix of amusement and horror. (A key part of the act was that Smigel was a terrible puppeteer—you often saw his arm or his head in the camera shot, and he couldn't help laughing at his own jokes.) The segment ended with a bunch of somber Westminster officials surrounding Triumph and the camera just before he gets thrown out.

So of course Conan sent Triumph back the next year—this

time "disguised" in a mustache and sombrero and calling himself Ed Bradley from *60 Minutes*. He interviewed a couple of handlers who got the joke and a couple more who clearly did not. There was another round of humping. You are going to be shocked to hear that he got thrown out again.

Much of the mocking in more recent years has been centered on how handlers dress. You don't have to poke around on the Internet very long to find message board posts like "Why do dog handlers wear ugly clothes?" (Which, as a female handler told me, is code for "Why do these women wear such ugly clothes?")

A lot of this stems from a simple fact: dog handlers have to run, or at least trot a little. That rules out stylish heels for female handlers (I saw one or two with low, wide heels). Most women in the fancy go with sort of a mullet approach: business above the knee, comfort below. A lot of black rubber-soled shoes like an older nurse might wear. Remember, handlers are on their feet all day. They also need shoes that provide a grip on all sorts of surfaces, from concrete to grass to dirt. The one thing they can't do in the show ring is fall. In 2021, in Westminster's agility competition—a separate event from the main dog show—a handler fell and nearly squished his Boston terrier named Ripple. The video got half a million views on YouTube. This is not how you want to get half a million views on YouTube.

There's a long-running debate among people in the fancy about outfits. One theory goes that handlers should dress as drab as possible so that all the attention is drawn to the dog. The opposing theory is that a handler should go with something bold so that it'll stick in the judge's memory. I saw one handler who had basically dressed as a piano: black pants, glittery white sport jacket, and one of those ties with piano keys. It'll be a long time before I forget that handler. But I can't remember a single thing about his dog.

It's not a fashion show, it's a dog show. Week to week, out in the clusters, you don't see many dazzling ensembles. But Westminster is different. At Westminster, Laura King is wearing a skirt suit a friend picked out for her. She looks great in it. It's reddish purple, laced with golden threads. Purple and gold are Westminster's official colors. It's a bit of subliminal advertising.

Striker had eight hours between winning his breed at Westminster and his next round, the Working Group. He spent some of it napping in the back of Betty White, which is kept at seventy-two degrees because that's the temperature he likes—a perk of being the lead dog. But he spent a lot of it being groomed. Again.

Show dogs spend more time being groomed than they do in the ring. Most of them spend more time being groomed than anything else in their waking life. The coat is a sign of the handler's skill as much as the dog's. A stray tangle or a matted spot is the sign of an amateur. This is where the analogy of dog show to beauty pageant hits the closest. These dogs are primped like a thousand Miss Tennessees.

Samoyeds like Striker require a shedding comb to draw out fur from the undercoat, plus a pin brush for tangles, plus a slicker brush to keep the coat shiny. If they also get a bath, they dry off under the blast of a special dryer, which is about halfway between a hair dryer for people and a leaf blower. The whole process takes three hours.

Before he started working with Laura in the States, Striker had already been showing in Canada with Judi Elford, the breeder who picked him from the litter as a puppy. Judi and Striker's other owners wanted to see what he could do in the bigger world of US shows. Judi handed him over to Laura at a show in Tallmadge, Ohio, on the first weekend of 2020. Two months later, COVID hit and shut down all dog shows for a while. Then they started coming back in places like Florida, where regulations weren't as strict. It was a dicey time in the fancy. Dog handlers like to pick and choose the shows they go to. Now they didn't have much choice. The shows were so scarce that they overflowed with dogs—three thousand dogs at a show that normally got just a thousand. All the best dogs came to every show. The competition was so much harder than it would normally have been for a dog just starting out in America. Laura noticed something, though. Striker *loved* it. He didn't win right away because he was too amped. But once she cooled him off just a little, he started racking up Best in Shows.

The bathing, the combing, the waiting—he's done it all now, hundreds of times. And he's won, dozens of times. So has Laura. She preps him and loads him into his crate atop a wheeled cart, and they head across the lawn toward the TV tent. All over the country, viewers are just tuning in. By the end of the night the thousands of dogs that started the show will be whittled down to one.

The night before, the Westminster judges had picked the winners of the first four groups: Hound, Toy, Non-Sporting, and Herding. Tonight starts with the final three groups—Sporting, Working, and Terrier—and then goes straight into Best in Show.

The show tent at Lyndhurst isn't to the scale of Madison

Square Garden, but there's still room for a couple thousand people in the bleachers. FOX Sports has rigged the tent with lights and cameras everywhere, including two cameras in the middle of the ring, hidden in toadstool-shaped casings so the dogs won't notice. It's a cool night but the AC is set to max. It's freezing inside. There's a brisk market at the concession stand for coffee and cocktails.

Laura and Striker and their team find a spot to set up backstage. The other dogs and handlers are crowded in, along with a caterer who does not have seem to have understood that there would be dogs around his food. It's a little chaotic back here.

The Sporting Group goes first and then clears the ring. In the back, the thirty-one dogs in the Working Group line up alphabetically by breed. Laura and Striker take their spot between the Saint Bernard and the Siberian husky.

Win this round and they make it to the final seven. Win this round and Striker has a shot to retire as not just a champion, but one of *the* champions.

From the other side of the wall, out in the main tent, announcer Michael LaFave says: "May we have the Working Group, please?"

The dogs stream into the arena. Laura and Striker come out near the end. Her head is down, looking at him. His head is up, looking at the lights.

FAMOUS WESTMINSTER DOG OWNERS, RANKED

#5

Tim McGraw

Country star married to another country star (Faith Hill). Won Best of Breed in 2023 with a Bracco Italiano* named Lepshi. It was the first year the breed was eligible for Westminster.

#4

Nellie Bly

Star journalist and adventurer from the late nineteenth century; in 1889, she completed an around-the-world voyage in seventy-two days, beating the fictional trip in the novel *Around the World in Eighty Days*. Entered her Maltese into Westminster in 1894.

*Bracco Italiano: Pointer developed in northern Italy as far back as the fifth century BC. Once a common gift from Italian leaders to VIPs of other countries. White with orange or brown patches; a beauty.

#3

Martha Stewart

Lifestyle icon, ex-con, and Snoop Dogg pal. Owned a Chow Chow named Genghis Khan that won Best of Breed in 2012. His son, Buddakan, won the same title in 2022.

#2

(tie) Lou Gehrig and Barry Bonds

Two of baseball's greatest. Gehrig, a Hall of Famer known for his streak of 2,130 consecutive games (and also for ALS, the disease nicknamed after him), owned a German shepherd named Afra of Cosalta that competed at Westminster in 1933. Bonds, the all-time home run leader (and symbol of the era of steroid allegations), owned a miniature schnauzer that competed in 2021.

#1

Patty Hearst

One of the most famous stories of the 1970s. Publishing heiress who was kidnapped by the Symbionese Liberation Army in 1974 and helped them rob a bank and commit other crimes that she may or may not have done voluntarily. Now a wife, mom, occasional actress, and socialite. Her Shih Tzu, Rocket, won the Toy Group in 2015; her French bulldogs, Tuggy and Rubi, won Best of Breed and Best of Opposite Sex in 2017.

4

CONFORMATION

Money can buy you a fine dog, but only love will make it wag its tail.

—Kinky Friedman

The tent is set up against a far wall, away from the crowd. The banner on the tent says INFINITY CANINE. The logo on the banner is a sperm cell swimming through a sideways eight. The slogan under the logo says: DOGS LOVE TO COME TO US!

Inside the tent, lounging in a crate, is a Borzoi* in heat. Her name is Marvel. She is the teaser bitch, the temptress, the milkshake that brings all the boys to the yard. Outside the tent is a handler with a foxhound straining at his lead. It is just about time to do business.

The business belongs to Stephanie Parker and Stacey Hathaway of Cary, North Carolina. They call themselves the Sperm Girls.

---

*Borzoi: Big, sleek, elegant hound with a head like needle-nose pliers and the prancing gait of a quarter horse. Once known as the Russian wolfhound ("borzoi" is rough Russian for "fast"). Featured in a hunting scene in *War and Peace*.

On this day Stephanie and her sister/assistant, Gina Hartless, have set up the tent in a cavernous convention center in suburban Philadelphia, home of the National Dog Show. Many TV viewers think the National Dog Show is Westminster, because the National Dog Show has a sweet TV slot on Thanksgiving Day. Since 2002 it has aired on NBC right after the Macy's parade and right before the NFL games start. NBC had been looking for something to replace *It's a Wonderful Life,* which was nose-diving in the ratings. Network exec Jon Miller had just seen *Best in Show* with his family and loved it so much that he watched it again by himself. He called the Kennel Club of Philadelphia, which runs the National Dog Show, and bought the rights to air the competition. The time slot makes it the most-watched dog show in America. Among the fancy, it's a big deal, but not quite Westminster. The feeling is more casual. Which makes it perfect for the Sperm Girls.

They go to eight or ten of the major dog shows every year, collecting dog semen samples for their clients. The process is simple: A dog enters the tent. The dog doesn't mount the teaser; he just gets a sniff. Sometimes all it takes is a pair of panties taken from a bitch in heat. Whatever gets the dog ready. When he is, one of the Sperm Girls steps in.

The collection is . . . manual.

"It's exactly what you're picturing at the moment," Stephanie says. "If you had told me in tech school that I would be doing this, I would have slapped you."

She asks me to step outside for a bit while she takes care of the waiting foxhound. He is in the tent for twenty-three minutes. Maybe I am seeing things, but I swear he leaves with a bounce in his step.

Infinity Canine will spin the foxhound's semen through a centrifuge to separate out the sperm. They'll test it for brucellosis— sort of a dog version of an STD—and then separate the sperm into straws, each one holding enough for an artificial insemination. Then they'll freeze the straws in liquid nitrogen in one of their tanks back in North Carolina, along with the samples of some three thousand other dogs. The company's show rate for the service is $275, which includes one year of storage. Some breeders store their dogs' sperm much longer. It can last pretty much forever. If a breeder winds up with an ideal dog, they can mate that dog—or at least what it left behind—with any number of bitches, long after the dog and everyone it ever knew have crossed the rainbow bridge.

People in Dogland will tell you the same line over and over: the purpose of a dog show is not to choose the most beautiful dog; the purpose is to identify the best breeding stock. Other competitions, like agility shows, measure a dog's skills. But the standard dog show—a show like Westminster—is a conformation show. The goal is to find the dog that conforms the closest to the ideal version of its breed. Conformity matters because purebred dog owners and breeders prize consistency. They want to know that the puppies they buy and sell will be as much as possible like their champion parents. Theoretically, conformation also produces dogs that can be counted on to do the work they were bred to do.

All this is both totally reasonable and complete bullshit.

Reasonable, because it makes sense that a successful dog has a good chance to produce more dogs just like it.

Bullshit, because the meaning of "success" means something completely different in Dogland than it does in the real world.

Modern breed standards are not about producing dogs that have a useful set of skills or a tireless work ethic. They're about creating supermodels.

A brief sampling, by breed, of flaws that can get a show dog disqualified:

Alaskan malamute: Blue eyes.

Fox terrier (smooth): Nose colored white or cherry, or spotted with either color.

Doberman pinscher: Overbite of more than three-sixteenths of an inch, or underbite of more than one-eighth inch.

Papillon: All white or not having any white.

Rottweiler: Any base color other than black.

Weimaraner: A "distinctly long coat."

Chesapeake Bay retriever: Coat that is curly or "with a tendency to curl all over the body."

Shetland sheepdog: Height of less than thirteen inches or more than sixteen inches.

Chihuahua: Weight of more than six pounds.

Dachshund: In the piebald pattern, having eyes partially or wholly blue; having a head that is more than 50 percent white; having white covering any portion of the ears, back, and front, or around the eyes; or being pure white with no body spots except on the head.

Rhodesian ridgeback: Ridgelessness.

(OK, that one seems fair.)

I could have made this list fifty times as long. Spend enough time reading breed standards and you wonder how any dogs ever qualify. The breed standard for the Chow Chow* alone is 2,213 words—longer than the Declaration of Independence and the Gettysburg Address combined. And if you breed Chow Chows, possibly more important.

Some breed standards have sound practical roots in dog genetics. Dogs, compared with humans, have fewer of the genetic on/off switches that control certain traits. That means each switch on a dog controls more variables. If you flip the switch for a certain eye color, for example, it might be the same switch that controls the length of the legs. Over generations, breeders noticed those tendencies and baked them into the breed standards, with the idea of making sure the dog had the physical tools it needed to do the work it was intended for.

But now most of the fine points are geared toward making the dog look its best—at least in the eyes of the specialty clubs that write (and rewrite) the breed standards. A show dog does move around the ring, and it's partly judged on its gait, but most of the breed standard centers on how the dog is supposed to look, from tooth to tail.

The simplest cases are docking and cropping. Those are euphemisms for cutting off a dog's tail or part of its ears. This has gone on for centuries, for some reasons that made sense (a hunting dog might injure its tail running through thick brush) and others that made no sense (a poor person's dog might have its tail docked to signify that it wasn't *permitted* to hunt).

---

*Chow Chow: Burly, lionlike Chinese dog with a distinctive blue tongue, acquired (the legend goes) by licking up pieces of sky that fell to Earth when the stars were created. Famous owners include Queen Victoria, Sigmund Freud, Georgia O'Keeffe, and Elvis.

The AKC recognizes about twenty breeds that require tail docking to meet the breed standard, and around sixty that require some form of ear cropping. The breed standard for the Doberman pinscher states it clearly: "Tail docked at approximately second joint . . . Ears normally cropped and carried erect." That "carried erect" part is especially interesting. A Doberman's ear flaps naturally cover the ear canal. To make them stand upright after they're cropped, they're taped in place for weeks until they stand up on their own. This makes for a bitter dose of irony: a perfect purebred Doberman, left alone, does not meet the Doberman breed standard. This is like saying Jennifer Lawrence would not really be beautiful unless she got a nose job.

All this is done when the dog is young, sometimes shortly after birth, like a circumcision. I guess the idea is if it's done early enough, the dog won't remember. Regardless, it's no longer done for function, especially in the dog-show world. It's completely about preserving the memory of what we think a particular dog is supposed to look like. Nostalgia with a scalpel.

And because of it, many dogs lose their tails—the most expressive part of their bodies. Dogs communicate so much with their tails: joy, curiosity, fear, excitement, confidence. It's like stealing their voice. The American Veterinary Medical Association opposes docking and cropping, and it's been banned in Australia, as well as in several countries in Europe. But here in Dogland, no one complains much.

Beyond the cruel cuts, current breed standards often lead dogs far off the path of what a given dog was originally designed to do. The *Washington Post* did a story back in 1991 on a herding clinic the AKC put on at a park in suburban DC. They took five sheep out into a field and then sent a bunch of supposed herding dogs after them. None of the dogs—including a German shepherd, a Hungarian puli,* and three types of sheepdog—had a damn clue what to do.

But they probably looked awesome not doing it.

There have been multiple lawsuits over the years from dog owners who didn't want the AKC to recognize their breeds, because a breed standard might push a dog away from its working roots. That *Washington Post* story came about because a vocal group of border collie owners didn't want the AKC deciding what a real border collie was. Owners of breeds already under the AKC umbrella found other reasons to protest. In 1994 the parent club for Labrador retrievers rewrote its breed standard to disqualify any dogs less than 22½ inches tall, and bitches less than 21½ inches. (Dog heights are generally measured at the withers, the high point of the shoulder.) This restriction disqualified thousands of smaller Labs from not just dog shows, but lucrative breeding fees. So a group of owners and breeders filed a class-action suit.

The AKC beat the Lab owners in court. But they had a harder time dealing with the folks who owned Jack Russell terriers, which makes sense if you've ever been around a Jack Russell terrier. (The dogs can be such assholes that even some of their fans call them "Jack Russell terrorists.") Jack Russell owners had their own breed

---

*Puli: One of the "dogs with dreads" whose fur forms thick cords (others include the Komondor and Bergamasco). Probably developed in Hungary sometime in the ninth century. A famous puli stray lived in an abandoned copper mine in Butte, Montana, until his death in 2003. Townspeople called him the Auditor, because he showed up when they least expected.

club, with standards meant to preserve the terrier's working-dog origins. They thought AKC recognition would diminish the breed. But a few rogue breeders split off, formed their own club, and persuaded the AKC to recognize the breed in 1997. The original breed club sued, and while it could not stop the AKC recognition, the suit did lead the AKC to take the Jack Russell name out of its mouth. The AKC now recognizes a dog that, to the untrained eye, is a Jack Russell terrier. But no! Its official name is a *Parson* Russell terrier. It's called that because John Russell, the Brit who created the breed in the late 1800s, was—you guessed it—a parson. What was essentially the same dog has now been split into two breeds with different standards. Parson Russells shine in the show ring. Jack Russells eat your couch.

All this talk of breed standards and genetic tweaking might make you a little queasy. Because this is the language of eugenics.

Eugenics—the idea that society benefits from a more pure gene pool—is part of what led the Nazis to kill six million Jews. It has led to various ethnic purges around the world. In the United States, it led health departments and hospitals in the twentieth century to sterilize tens of thousands of women deemed unfit to have children. Usually those women were some combination of poor, Black, and/or mentally disabled. (In Charlotte, North Carolina, where I live, the architect of the sterilization program from the '40s into the '70s was a county welfare director named Wallace Kuralt. Charles Kuralt, the journalist who did the famous "On the Road" segments for CBS, was his son.)

It's eugenics when we do it to other humans. When we do it

to animals and plants, we call it selective breeding. It's nothing new. We have selectively bred everything from corn to cattle for thousands of years. Today, science allows us to go directly into organic DNA and produce not just helpful innovations (seedless watermelons), but also more disturbing concoctions. In the summer of 2023, the United States Department of Agriculture cleared the sale of lab-created chicken that does not come from an actual living chicken. It makes sense to start there, considering how many things taste like chicken.

What we've done to dogs, as a whole, adds up to one of the most successful selective breeding programs in human history. But because dogs are closer to us than any other creatures, it can also feel like eugenics. Apes are more like us when it comes to DNA, but gorillas and chimps are something we go see at the zoo. Dogs live with us, sleep in our beds, curl up on the couch with us to watch a movie. For many people they're more like roommates than pets.

It might not be good for your sleep to think too hard about exactly how we ended up with all these dog breeds to begin with. At nearly every step, from the first moment humans started breeding dogs, we have decided what a dog would and would not be. We have created breeds that never would have happened naturally, and constantly tinkered with the ones that did. We have built dogs to fit our needs, our moods, our jobs, our living spaces, our ideas on what they should eat and how they should behave. And, most obviously, how they should look.

That, by God, is conformation.

And sometimes, when dog owners get exactly the dog they want, they refuse to let go. Barbra Streisand famously cloned two puppies from the cell tissue of her Coton de Tulear* named Saman-tha, who died in 2017 after she and Streisand had been together for fourteen years. Streisand sent the cells to a Texas company called ViaGen, which charges $50,000 to clone a dog. (Same price for a cat.) "You can clone the look of a dog, but you can't clone the soul," Streisand wrote in an essay for the *New York Times*. "Still, every time I look at their faces, I think of Samantha . . . and smile."

Maybe that still sounds strange to you. But Streisand will never own the title of Strangest Dog Cloner, not as long as Javier Milei is around. Milei is an economist and right-wing politician in Argen-tina who is best known there for his five cloned mastiffs—Murray, Milton, Robert, Lucas, and Conan. The first four are named for his favorite economists. The fifth is for *Conan the Barbarian*.

All five were cloned from Milei's earlier mastiff, also named Conan, who died in 2017. He arranged the cloning through a company called—my apologies in advance—PerPETuate.

None of that is the weird part.

The weird part is that Milei considers the mastiffs to be his political advisers, via a mystic who serves as a go-between. (Mur-ray, for example, gives advice on the economy.) If you think this in any way disqualifies him from office, welcome back to Earth from wherever you have spent the past few years. In November 2023, Milei was elected president of Argentina.

*Coton de Tulear: Named for its white fur and its origin in Tuléar, now known as Toli-ara, a coastal city on the island of Madagascar. The legend goes that the breed originated when a handful of small white dogs swam to shore after a shipwreck as far back as the fifteenth century. Pirates were possibly involved. The dogs lived there in isolation until the 1960s, when French tourists brought some home and introduced them to the rest of the world.

• • •

Some recent research on wolves has shown that they don't travel in packs nearly as much as we once thought. Instead, the basic unit is a family—a mother, a father, and pups. Left alone, that's how many animals organize themselves. It's how dogs would, if we let them. But one of the ways we have exerted control over dogs is by removing them from their natural families. Every dog in someone's home has a mother and father they may have never known. One of the reasons dogs are special is how well they have been able to substitute their human parents for their natural ones.

At my house, we have noticed how this plays out with our family cat. He came to us when my mother-in-law moved into a retirement home in 2019. She had taken him in as a feral kitten after somebody dropped off a litter at a vet's office. As far as we know, he never knew his parents. He's almost four years old as I write this, and he has mellowed a good bit, partly with the help of a behavioral consultant, partly through Prozac (it was either him or us). But he was hell to live with for the first couple of years. He would howl and bang on the hallway door at three thirty or four every morning until I got up or my wife, Alix, did. Eventually my mother-in-law moved in with us, and she blissfully slept through the madness. But when she got up, the cat would snarl and swipe at her, like he was pissed that she started this whole mess. She had just called him Kitty, but we ended up naming him Jack Reacher, after the Lee Child action hero who loves a good fight and never backs down.

Would Jack have had a different personality if he'd grown up with his natural cat family? Probably. Sometimes Joann, my mother-in-law, suggests that the way to calm Jack down is to get a couple more cats. A lot of animal experts recommend the same thing. All I can see in my mind is catfights on the kitchen floor. For now I'm exercising my veto power. One hellion in the house is enough.

But it's made me think about what it must be like for any animal who lives with people. The vast majority of them are orphans. Even if they don't carry the same emotional baggage a human would, at the very least they missed out on some of the natural instructions a parent would teach them.

Not only that, but many dogs spend big chunks of their time alone. Separation anxiety can drive some dogs crazy; they whine, moan, destroy furniture, pee on the floor. Sometimes the problem is something that happens along with the separation—for example, some owners put their dogs in a crate before they leave, and the dog might be anxious about the crate more than the owner's absence. But the separation itself matters, too. It makes more sense if you think about it like a dog. As humans, when we leave the house, we know we're coming back. A dog might not have that same kind of linear thought, or the same concept of "later." It's possible some dogs think that when you leave, you're leaving for good. And that can scare them to death, if for no other reason than you're the one who feeds them.

But most dogs, either through nature or nurture, have defeated separation anxiety. In fact they've managed to overcome all the strangeness humans have put them through. This is the one breed standard that applies to all dogs, purebred or mutt: the ability to adapt to how humans live. By that standard, most dogs are champions. It's not the kind of conformation measured in height or eye color. To quote Liam Neeson, sort of, it's a particular set of skills, acquired over a very long career. It's a far more difficult kind of conformation, and dogs have mastered it.

They are so good at it that we find ourselves conforming to them, too.

Westminster's symbolic ideal is a pointer originally named Don. He was a British dog, imported to America in 1876 by the men who would put on the first Westminster the following year. They knew him only through his reputation and a couple of pictures. He was never intended to be a show dog. Club members had agreed not to enter their own dogs in the show. Don was a hired stud, brought in to improve the club's breeding stock.

Once he arrived, club members fell in love. There's a strain of writing about dogs and dog shows that tends to value understatement. Westminster's website describes Don as having been "a handsome lemon and white dog, with a fine head and especially good body." For a group of men in the 1870s, that description was basically a Nicholas Sparks novel. Their new name for him gave the game away: Sensation. He visited Westminster as an exhibition dog and fans flocked to him. His picture appeared in magazines and newspapers across the country. Sensation quickly became Westminster's unofficial symbol, and eventually its official one. A rendering of him frozen at full point is embossed on the cover of the Westminster catalog. When I went to the 2020 show, one of the first things I saw was a larger-than-life statue of Sensation surrounded by velvet ropes.

Sensation wasn't perfect, but the idea of him is perfect.

Perfection, or something close to it, is the target for every show dog. It's baked into the rules. Which marks the biggest difference between Dogland and the real world. Because in the real world, what most dog lovers love most about dogs is their imperfections.

In 2015, Matt Nelson—a freshman at Campbell University in North Carolina, home of the Fighting Camels—started a Twitter account called WeRateDogs, with the handle @dog_rates. His first rating was of a friend's collie with one white eye and one brown eye:

> Here we have a Japanese Irish Setter. Lost eye in Vietnam (?). Big
> fan of relaxing on stair. 8/10 would pet.

Not a great joke, or even one that makes a lot of sense—the dog looked neither Japanese nor Irish—but it was a start.

Nelson had been playing around with social media, trying to figure out something that might draw a big following, and he soon realized a couple of things. One, every dog he featured should be rated at least 10/10, and most of them should be something like 12/10 or 13/10, which is mathematically impossible but emotionally accurate. And two, people *really* loved pictures of dogs.

As of fall 2023, WeRateDogs had 9.2 million followers on Twitter, 3.2 million on Instagram, and 2.1 million on TikTok.

Nelson went to college to become a golf teacher. Now he runs the WeRateDogs empire, which includes a book and a yearly calendar, plus shirts and hats and a sticker that says (in lowercase) "tell your dog i said hi." I see that sticker on somebody's car at least once a week. I always promise to say hi even though we do not currently have a dog.

There's also a spin-off Twitter feed called Thoughts of Dog, which is a cross between Dadaist poetry and Tony Robbins:

> i had a long talk. with my fren. about how to spot. a fake ball throw. the optimal strategy. is to follow the ball. with your eyes. instead of your heart

The major draw of WeRateDogs is still the stream of dog photos sent in by fans. The dogs often look so odd or act so goofy that Nelson has a recurring gag where he reminds his followers that he only rates dogs, and not (for example, paired with a video of a dog mooing) Golden-Toed Tiny Cows.

The point of all this is that nobody on WeRateDogs pays any attention to breed standards. Most of the dogs are clearly mutts. They often walk with a cockeyed gait or have a few teeth short of a mouthful. Many of them are dogs that were injured or abandoned and need surgery or some other kind of care. Nelson started a nonprofit called the 15/10 Foundation for those dogs. When he posts one of them on his feeds, followers pay for their care in a matter of minutes.

You never see the dogs on WeRateDogs in a show ring. They're doing stuff normal dogs do—dozing on the sofa, running on the beach, scarfing ice cream. Sometimes the joke is in the pose, like the one featuring a golden retriever from Richmond. He's sitting in a Toyota with a concerned look, front paws perched on the steering wheel. The caption:

This is Riley. He's trying to parallel park for the first time. Really wishes he had learned to drive first. 13/10

Nelson has a genius for pairing the photo and the one-liner, but he's just doing what so many other dog owners do—celebrating the day-to-day goofiness in most dog lovers' lives. Nearly everyone who owns a dog has a camera roll dominated by dog photos. And the best ones are almost always the ones that aren't carefully posed. They're the ones with the dog's tongue hanging out, or its nose mashed up against the camera lens. Dogs being dogs. Mostly, mutts being mutts.

According to the Humane Society of the United States, more than half the dogs in America are some sort of mixed breed. That's still a much lower percentage than the rest of the world. In many countries there are basically no purebreds at all—most of the dogs are "village dogs" that roam free and don't belong to anyone in particular.

Two brothers, Adam and Ryan Boyko, started getting samples from some of those dogs as part of their research into the history of dogs. They eventually founded a company called Embark (note the pun) that does DNA testing for dogs. Some of their customers just want to know their dog's genetic makeup. In the long run, the Boykos hope their collection of DNA samples will help breeders and scientists figure out ways to help dogs live longer.

I caught up with Ryan Boyko while he was at the National Dog Show. It was sort of an odd place for him, because the dog show is a place where breed means everything, and to him it means practically nothing.

So what does it mean to be a purebred dog? I asked him. He laughed.

"The question is a fine question in the abstract," he said. "The problem is that people, the audience of people—humanity or at least Western community—think of dogs in terms of breed. Breed is a really weird artificial construct, or human-created construct, that has relevance for only a tiny fraction of dogs that ever existed in the US or the world."

For Boyko, learning anything interesting from dogs by studying purebreds would be like trying to learn about human DNA by studying only the British royal family. There's just not enough diversity to gain anything useful.

We'll get more into what breeding has done to some types of dogs a little later. For now, consider this: Do you think the dogs care?

My experience is that a horny dog is willing to hump anything at all, including your leg or the dining room table. As fun as the Sperm Girls are—and they are tremendous fun—they illustrate one of the sad parts in the life of a show dog: because their breeding is so carefully controlled, they rarely, if ever, have sex.

One of the many things we don't know about dogs is whether that bothers them. But we can imagine. Because we know our own powerful desire to mate. That desire has led humanity, by and large, to be one giant mixed breed. Race is more a social construct than a scientific one anyway, but still we cross every genetic boundary and throw our DNA in a blender. We are the opposite of conformation. We are the ultimate nonconformists. And while the occasional Nazi comes along to argue otherwise, it seems to have worked out pretty well for humanity.

This is one of the ironies of Dogland. Dogs, through centuries of human intervention, are able to meet breed standards in a way their owners and handlers never could. The dogs are all purebreds. The people, they're all mutts.

The Samoyed breed standard is one of the longer ones—about 1,600 words. Like most breed standards, it's a mix of technical details and vibes. "Length of leg from the ground to the elbow should be approximately 55 percent of the total height at the withers," the standard says in one place. In another: "The Samoyed, being essentially a working dog, should present a picture of beauty, alertness and strength, with agility, dignity and grace." A show-quality Samoyed can't have blue eyes or a barrel chest. It has to have a thick coat, including "protective growth of hair between the toes." Under the heading "Disposition," it says: "Intelligent, gentle, loyal, adaptable, alert, full of action, eager to serve, friendly but conservative, not distrustful or shy, not overly aggressive." That's a hell of a lot of boxes to check. I don't know many people who fit that description.

I asked Laura King once to describe where Striker fails to meet the Samoyed breed standard. She could think of just one thing.

"He has a little piece of color that's missing," she said. "On the inside—not on the outside of his lip, but on the inside of his lip right here on the off side."

(A quick detour: The "off side" is the right side of a dog. The left side is called the "show side." That's because the left side is the one the judge can see from the middle of the ring as the dogs trot around the ring counterclockwise. Like NASCAR drivers, show dogs always turn left.)

The point is, a tiny patch of discolored lip that a normal

human being would never notice is about all that separates Striker from physical perfection.

It reminded me of a Nathaniel Hawthorne short story from the 1840s called "The Birth-Mark." It's about a scientist who marries a beautiful woman but becomes obsessed with removing her only blemish—a birthmark on her cheek. After several experiments, he finally concocts a potion that works. The birthmark fades. And at the moment it vanishes, the young woman dies.

If Striker didn't have that little discoloration on his lip, would he exist at all? It's not exactly the sort of existential question they talk about much in Dogland. The existential questions there tend to be about the best brand of shampoo. But like the aspiration to wealth and status, the yearning for perfection hangs over every dog show, because so many of the dogs are so nearly perfect.

Or, at least, nearly perfect in the eyes of the fancy. But they use a different filter than the rest of us.

I should finish this thought by making clear that purebred dogs can be goofballs, too.

Years ago I went to see a man about a dog. His name was Bob Plott, and he's one of the last family members who breeds Plott hounds. The breed started with five dogs brought over from Germany in 1750 by Johannes Plott, who settled in what is now North Carolina. Plott hounds became renowned hunting dogs, unafraid of bears or boars. They are the North Carolina state dog.

Bob took me out to see the dogs in the pens behind his house. They were purebred Plotts, baying and whooping. Most of them had the breed's classic black-and-brown brindle coat. Gorgeous dogs. If Bob had turned his head, I would've taken a couple home.

As he was describing them, he told a story about one named

Bud. In the winter sometimes the dogs' water bowls froze, and Bob would have to go out in the morning and knock out the chunks of ice. Bud loved the chunks of ice. One of his favorite things was burying the ice like some dogs bury a bone. Only problem was, Bud did not grasp the concept of melting. So later in the day, when he went to dig up his treat and it was gone, Bud would be furious. *WHO STOLE MY ICE?*

Now that's a perfect dog.

It struck me, watching Striker under the lights at Westminster, that he was basically the same color as the lights. Or, put another way, he had the same absence of color. That brilliant whiteness was hard to stare at sometimes. Striker left an afterimage in my eyes when I looked away. That absence was part of his presence.

It also reminded me of a projector screen, the kind a teacher might pull down at the front of a classroom. The image was on the nose because Striker was so white, but it applies to all dogs. People project so many things onto their dogs. Because a dog can't talk back, we're free to invent conversations with them. We get to play both parts and imagine not only what we want to say to them but how they would respond. There are so many *New Yorker* dog cartoons that I love, but my current favorite is one by Jason Adam Katzenstein. A police officer has stopped a car that appears to be driven by a friendly Lab. The dog reaches through the window and the officer takes its paws in his hands, saying: "Do you know why I pulled you over? Do you? Do you? Yes, you do."

When psychologists talk about projection, it's usually got a negative meaning—for example, someone with self-esteem issues might bully others to tamp down that feeling. But when it comes to dogs, projection involves all kinds of feelings. It can be as simple as a lonely person needing to talk to anyone, about anything, and their dog is the nearest creature around.

It's another form of conformation—one where we imagine the dogs in our lives as the partners we want them to be, in a world we can control. One of the most enjoyable things about a show like Westminster is imagining those dogs in your house. It's easy to conjure the image in your mind. With Striker, though, it's different. His near-perfect brightness can be more than the eye can handle. It can be a bit like staring at the sun.

DOGS IN ART, RANKED

#5

Stanley and Boodgie

Dachshunds belonging to British artist David Hockney, who painted dozens of portraits of them starting in the 1990s. He set up easels all over his house so he could capture them wherever they happened to be—based on the paintings, usually sleeping.

#4

Lump

Another dachshund, one that Pablo Picasso adopted as his muse after borrowing him (for six years!) from photographer David Douglas Duncan. The first day they met, Picasso painted Lump on a dinner plate. He later incorporated the dog into many of his sketches and studies.

#3
Balloon Dog

Sculptor Jeff Koons has made several versions in different colors, sizes, and materials. *Balloon Dog (Orange)* sold in 2013 for $58.4 million. A small blue porcelain version (valued at $42,000) shattered at a 2023 art fair in Miami when a patron tapped it with her finger and knocked it over. A virtual tribute called *Yellow Dog with Cone* is a prize players can buy in *Grand Theft Auto Online*.

#2
The dog at the Last Supper

Many artists painted versions of the Last Supper; Leonardo da Vinci's interpretation is just the most famous. Paolo Veronese's rendering from 1573 got the artist in trouble for making Christ's last meal look like a hell of a party. The painting includes jesters, drunken Germans, some guy with a nosebleed . . . and a dog, sitting quietly in front of Jesus's table, watching a cat lounge under the tablecloth. Italian authorities demanded that Veronese make changes—including replacing the dog with Mary Magdalene. Instead Veronese dropped *The Last Supper* from the title, renamed it *Feast in the House of Levi,* and left in all the fun stuff. It now hangs in the Gallerie dell'Accademia in Venice.

#1
Dogs playing poker

Actually a series of eighteen paintings made by Cassius Marcellus Coolidge between 1894 and 1910—most of them for a cigar company's ad campaign. The most famous (with one bulldog passing another an ace via his left rear paw) is 1903's *A Friend in Need.* The first painting, called *Poker Game,* sold at a Sotheby's auction in 2015 for $658,000.

5

THE TROUBLE WITH FRENCHIES

The question is not, Can they *reason?* nor, Can they *talk?* but, Can they *suffer?*

—Jeremy Bentham, *An Introduction to the Principles of Morals and Legislation*

It is even harder than you might expect to be Lady Gaga's dog walker.

Ryan Fischer discovered this on the night of February 24, 2021. He had gone out for a stroll with Asia, Koji, and Gustav—Gaga's three French bulldogs.

They were walking through a neighborhood in West Hollywood when a white Nissan Altima pulled up and two men jumped out of the back seat. They grabbed at the dogs. Fischer tried to fight the men off. One of them pulled a gun and shot Fischer in the chest. The men got back in the car and drove off with Koji and Gustav. Asia had escaped in the struggle; she ran over to Fischer, who was bleeding on the sidewalk. A neighbor's doorbell camera captured the whole thing on video.

This was a story created in a lab especially for TMZ. They did not disappoint.

"LADY GAGA DOGNAPPING, SHOOTING MAY HAVE BEEN GANG INITATION"

"LADY GAGA DOG ABDUCTION: DOG WALKERS EYEING GUNS, JIU-JITSU FOR PROTECTION DURING WALKS"

"LADY GAGA DOG WALKER TESTIFIES HE HIT ATTACKERS WITH CHAMPAGNE BOTTLE"

Koji and Gustav turned out to be fine. A woman turned them in to police a couple days later, saying she had found them tied to a pole. But two months after that, police arrested the woman along with four other people—three men accused of committing the dognapping, two others as accessories.

Here are some other things that happened during the course of the story:

- James Jackson, who was convicted of shooting Fischer, was sentenced to twenty-one years in prison—but only after being accidentally released before his trial, then recaptured four months later.
- The woman who turned in the dogs failed in her lawsuit against Lady Gaga for a $500,000 reward Gaga had offered even though the reward was supposedly "no questions asked."
- Ryan Fischer rented a van and drove cross-country on what he called a healing tour. Then he started a GoFundMe to cover his expenses when the van broke down.

You can see why I am reluctant to describe anything in this case as "the weirdest part." But here is one very weird part: the dognappers apparently had no idea the dogs they were napping belonged to one of the most famous people on the planet.

In fact, technically, they weren't dognappers—they were dog-*jackers*. They weren't looking to nab celebrities' dogs for ransom. They were just cruising the streets for French bulldogs to steal.

Because these days, if you are criminally inclined, a French bulldog is very much worth stealing.

In 2022, French bulldogs pulled off a feat more startling than winning any dog show: they became the most popular breed in America.

This ended the epic run of the Labrador retriever, which had been the top dog for thirty-one years straight. The last time Labs weren't number one, Miley Cyrus had not been born and Jerry Garcia was still alive. Back then, French bulldogs didn't even make AKC's top seventy-five breeds. But over the past decade they've surged up the list. The AKC picks the top breed based on new registrations every year. And in 2022, nearly one in seven registered dogs was a Frenchie—more than 108,000 in all.

If you don't know French bulldogs well, and maybe even if you do, you might rightly be wondering: *What the hell?*

I will approach this delicately, not just because many people love Frenchies, but also because our next-door neighbors *really* love Frenchies, and often wheel their adorable dogs around the neighborhood in a stroller. (Hey, y'all!) So let me say this in a positive way: French bulldogs were created to do absolutely nothing. And they are so damn good at it.

Their history begins in—I am not making this up—the lace-making industry in nineteenth-century England, specifically around Nottingham. Lacemaking was a seated job, and the ladies who made lace in Nottingham started bringing toy bulldogs to work to rest in their laps. Then the Industrial Revolution came along, and somebody developed machines to do the work. The ladies lost their jobs. But it turned out that France still valued handmade lace, and so a group of them moved there. They brought their toy bulldogs with them, and some of them bred the dogs with local pugs and terriers. Eventually the French bulldog emerged. They became especially popular among Parisian hookers, who enjoyed them as companions between their other sessions of companionship.

The surge in American popularity isn't linked to any one thing. Lots of celebrities own Frenchies, but none of the dogs themselves are famous (my favorite is the late Carrie Fisher's Frenchie, Gary Fisher, whose tongue perpetually dangles from the side of his mouth like a half-chewed cigar). They just fit a lot of Americans' lifestyles. They're small and comfortable indoors, so they're good for apartments and condos. They need attention but don't have to be walked for miles every day. They get into mischief but aren't likely to destroy your living room. They are, and have always been meant to be, the lappiest of lapdogs.

The French novelist Colette described her Frenchie as "an adorable creature whose face looked like a frog's that had been sat upon." In other words, the definition of "so ugly they're cute."

But here is why a band of criminals thought it was worth their while to become Frenchie dogjackers: French bulldogs are expensive as hell.

The AKC has a marketplace where you can browse puppies for sale from breeders across the country. When I scanned the Frenchies, the cheapest puppy available ran about $2,000. The price went up as the pedigree got stronger. One pair of puppies was selling for $9,000 apiece. A *New York Times* story from 2022 featured a breeder who said certain puppies could go for *$30,000.*

Why would a puppy—even the most popular puppy in America—cost as much as a new Honda Accord?

To get into that requires talking about some of the things that make French bulldogs different. And getting into *that* requires talking about other, similar dogs that are different in the same ways. It also requires looking hard at what people really want from dogs, and how the dog-show world reflects and contributes to those desires, and how some dogs suffer as a result.

One reason Frenchies cost so much is simple biology: French bulldogs can't have many babies. That's the inevitable result of how they were bred and constructed.

Frenchies have big heads, wide shoulders, and narrow hips. For a pregnant bitch, that is trouble from back to front. The narrow hips mean there's not much room for puppies. So a normal litter is three puppies, compared with six for a beagle or seven for a corgi or eight for a Great Dane. The big heads and wide shoulders mean that puppies often won't fit through the birth canal. About 80 percent of all Frenchies are born via C-section. That limits the number of litters before the mother wears out.

That top-heaviness also makes it hard for a male Frenchie to mount a mate and hold her in place. So most pregnancies occur through artificial insemination. To sum up: Frenchies generally don't get laid, they don't produce many babies, and when they do, it's an ordeal.

This sounds miserable for the dogs. But for breeders, it tips the law of supply and demand in their favor. The supply is always going to be low. And if the demand is high, like it is now, the price keeps going up.

It's important to remember that none of this had to happen this way. The shape of a French bulldog is a human invention. Breeders in the nineteenth century tinkered with regular bulldogs until they ended up with miniature versions. Then those dogs were blended with other small dogs to create the Frenchie. There was even a debate between American and European breeders about how a Frenchie's ears should look. The Europeans bred their dogs to have "rose ears"—ones that flop over, like rose petals. American breeders preferred "bat ears" that stay upright and erect. The Americans eventually won, at least on this side of the ocean. According to the AKC breed standard for Frenchies, anything but bat ears is a disqualification at a dog show.

Remember why breed standards exist in the first place. They're supposed to keep the essential character of the dog intact *so it can do the job it was made to do*. As far as I know, there are no studies that prove bat ears (or rose ears, for that matter) make a Frenchie a better lapdog. It's just what some breeders decided the dog should look like. And it means floppy-eared Frenchies, no matter how otherwise perfect they might be, never see the show ring.

In the end, though, the ears aren't that big a deal. That smushy frogface, though—that matters a lot. It's the feature that defines the Frenchie, the thing people love about them more than any other. But that face, for a Frenchie, is a literal killer.

Here's a Word of the Day for you: "brachycephalic." It means short-headed, or flat-faced. Several dog breeds share the characteristic, but it's most prominent in bulldogs of all kinds, including Frenchies.

Think of a more classically shaped dog—a Lab, or a greyhound. They have long noses, long jawlines, long airways. There's a lot of bone structure and soft tissue that helps a dog breathe. Brachycephalic dogs look like they ran face-first into a brick wall. All that bone and tissue is mashed together. Most brachycephalic dogs have a dangerous combination: some parts are too small (narrowed nostrils and tracheas) and other parts are too big (oversized tongues, soft palates that block the windpipe). Vets combine those issues into the acronym BOAS, for brachycephalic obstructive airway syndrome. Some Frenchie lovers find it adorable that they snore while they sleep and snort while awake. Gary Fisher looks cute with his tongue constantly hanging out. But those are byproducts of a terribly damaged respiratory system.

The Dutch government announced in 2023 that it planned to ban ownership of twelve breeds of flat-faced dogs, including Frenchies. Other European countries have discussed restrictions. But a large part of dog breeding happens outside the boundaries—geographical and ethical. Puppy mills abound all over the world. Some are mostly legit and might sell dogs that don't meet strict breed standards. The scale slides down from there into true horrors. In 2020, inspectors in Canada found five hundred puppies in the cargo hold of a flight from Ukraine. Some reports said all the puppies were Frenchies; other accounts said there were multiple breeds. The puppies were meant to be resold in Canada. At least thirty-eight of them died on the flight.

The life of a show dog is a different universe. You generally don't see Frenchies in distress at dog shows, because the selection process weeds out all but the healthiest dogs. As Laura and Striker traveled the circuit leading up to Westminster 2022, the top show dog in the country was a Frenchie from Oklahoma named Winston. (Props to his team for acknowledging that all Frenchies look like Winston Churchill.) Winston looked robust as he trotted around the ring. He appeared to have great cardio. But of course he would—he was at the top of the pyramid of all the dogs in his breed. He was about as perfect as a Frenchie gets.

For Frenchies with less pristine genes, life demands a lot.

They've been bred for big round eyes that make them prone to infections. The wrinkles in their faces develop rashes. They wear out fast, especially in the heat. They get old before their time.

In general, the bigger the dog, the more likely it is to die young. The Irish wolfhound—the tallest AKC breed—has a normal life span of just six to eight years. Great Danes, seven to ten. Most purebreds live somewhere between ten and fourteen years. (If you hate your cousin's Chihuahua, I have bad news: they often make it to eighteen.) Frenchies, even though they're small dogs, generally live just ten to twelve years. A UK study from 2022 skewed even worse—of all the purebred and crossbred dogs the researchers studied, Frenchies had the shortest expected life span.

It seems odd that a dog that doesn't live very long—and tends to have medical issues along the way—should be the most popular dog in America. Most stories about the Frenchie boom center on how they're easy to handle and thoroughly entertaining.

(Frenchies are big on Instagram and TikTok.) But there's another reason that people in the dog world don't like to talk much about. One of the few people I've seen say it clearly is Alexandra Horowitz, the dog cognition expert who has written several books about how dogs understand the world. She put it this way in an interview with Vox:

"We've bred them to look more like us."

Go find a picture of a Frenchie now, with that in mind.

Look at the wide-set eyes.

The flattened nose.

The mouth that can form a facsimile of a smile.

The ears that stick out instead of fold in.

Even their body shape plays into it. Most dogs look awkward on their hind legs, which is what makes it funny when you try to "dance" with them. But stand a Frenchie on its hind legs and the proportions can look eerily human. Everybody knows a short stocky guy with a big personality. An upright Frenchie gives off a big Danny DeVito vibe.

Part of the appeal of Frenchies is that they can't do what other dogs do. They can't jump up and steal a steak off the kitchen counter. They can't chase a squirrel for a mile through the woods. They prefer to hang out on the couch for TV and a belly rub. They're the perfect dog for a sedentary society. If they had opposable thumbs, they would definitely spend all day scrolling on their phones.

"So God created man in his own image," says Genesis 1:27 (KJV), and the Frenchie is the greatest proof of man as the god of the dog. We shrank an ordinary dog to fit in the lap of lace ladies, then we mashed its face to remind us of us, and then we were so well pleased that we made it the most popular dog in America. While at the same time, with every step, making its life harder and shorter.

And sometimes ours as well.

In February 2023, a seventy-six-year-old breeder named Lonnie Ray arranged to sell a Frenchie puppy for $2,500. He agreed to meet the buyer in the parking lot of a KFC in Bishopville, South Carolina. Ray was wary of parking-lot transactions, so he brought a friend along. But when they got there, they were swarmed by several attackers. The dogjackers shot Ray three times, shot at his friend but missed, and took the puppy. Ray died an hour later at a local hospital. Police arrested two men for his killing and expected to make more arrests. The Frenchie is still missing.

It's not just Frenchies. Pugs, Cavalier King Charles spaniels, boxers—they've all been bred for flat faces, and they all labor to breathe.

But it's the regular bulldog—what some folks call the English bulldog—that hits closest to home for me. Because I am a Georgia Bulldog—a graduate of the university, and a lifelong fan.

In January 2023, I was watching the college football national championship with one of my old roommates and his wife at their home in South Carolina. Our Dawgs were routing Texas Christian at SoFi Stadium in Los Angeles. They were about to win their second straight national title. We were already ordering BACK-TO-BACK merch online.

By the middle of the third quarter, it was 45–7 and the

announcers had run out of football things to talk about. So they shifted to a reliable segment in any Bulldogs game: the dog himself.

"Shout-out to Uga X, who's nine years old," said Chris Fowler, the play-by-play man for ESPN. "It was just too long for him to make the flight, so he's back in Athens checking it out."

A video feed showed somebody pulling a jersey onto Uga X. The dog turned to watch a TV showing the game. Underneath the TV was a Georgia license plate that said MASCOT.

"I was very disappointed to hear that the big man was not gonna be out here," said color commentator Kirk Herbstreit. "But at least he's enjoying it at home."

Fowler: "You know that bulldogs are not easy to fly long distances . . . They have the breathing problems, as you well know as a dog lover."

Herbstreit: "I thought somebody might drive him out. But everything seems to be handled out here at 45–7."

It was a deft couple of minutes of TV, a way to fill time in a blowout. (The final was 65–7. Go Dawgs.) But it was notable for two things. One, it was rare that Uga would stay home for such a big game. And two, Fowler told an uncomfortable truth on the air: *They have the breathing problems.*

Normally, no one mentions this when Georgia plays. There's always a shot meant for laughs of Uga on the sideline, hanging out in his custom doghouse. It can be hot in the South well into October, so even though the doghouse is air-conditioned, sometimes he's sacked out on a five-pound bag of ice. Still, he's often panting.

Uga X was, as you might have deduced, the tenth bulldog to take the name. It started in 1956 with a puppy that belonged to a law student from Savannah named Sonny Seiler and his wife, Cecelia. It was a belated wedding present. A friend suggested the name Uga, pronounced *Uh-guh*. Seiler decided to take the puppy to Georgia's home opener, and Cecelia made a red jersey for the dog to wear. The sports information director noticed the dog drawing a crowd. Seiler (who died in 2023) and his family have been in charge of the Uga bloodline ever since.

Over the years, Uga has accumulated as much lore as the Georgia players and coaches. Vince Dooley, who spent twenty-five years as the Georgia head coach, once told me the story of how Uga wandered out onto Vanderbilt's brand-new field during a practice and took a dump on the fifty-yard line. He also remembered a yearly ride in the Savannah Saint Patrick's Day parade with whichever Uga happened to be serving at the moment. He learned after a couple of parades not to get caught downwind of the dog.

One of the iconic moments in Georgia football history happened in the Georgia-Auburn game in 1996. Auburn receiver Robert Baker caught a touchdown pass, and his momentum carried him toward where Uga V was standing on the sideline with his handler, the Seilers' son, Charles. As Baker got close, Uga lunged at his crotch. Baker danced away as Charles yanked on the leash and Uga V's jaws snapped at air. What could have been a disaster (and probably the end of Uga roaming the sidelines) instead became a moment of self-actualization for Georgia fans: the dog itself had become a proxy of us, snarling at a rival, showing off its fighting spirit. Photos and paintings of that moment still hang in bars and man caves all over the state.

A quick joke, one I first heard from the Atlanta humorist Lewis

Grizzard: Two Georgia fans are sitting in the stands as the game is getting ready to start. Uga leads the team onto the field, then plops down in the grass and starts vigorously licking his privates.

The first fan laughs and says: "Damn, I wish I could do that."

The second fan turns to him in shock and says: "Man, that dog would bite you . . ."

Lots of dogs have been dealt bad hands over the centuries, but bulldogs might have fared the worst. They got their name from the barbaric sport of bullbaiting, a popular entertainment in England and Ireland for a couple hundred years through the early 1800s. It was born from a practical purpose: farmers needed dogs that could hold a bull still to keep it from wandering off. Some devious mind figured out that people might pay to see that battle, and might pay even more to bet on the dog or the bull. Before long they were holding the shows in arenas. A bull would be tethered to a stake with a rope. An assistant would stuff pepper into the bull's nose to get it good and mad. (Speaking of being dealt a bad hand, imagine having the job of bull nose pepper stuffer.) Then a dog would be set loose with the goal of latching on to the bull's snout and pinning it to the ground. (The third bad job in this equation: being the bull.) Several types of dogs were used in bullbaiting, but what became known as the bulldog—a dog built low to the ground, with powerful jaws—turned out to excel at the brutal job. It came with a heavy price. A bull would often kill several dogs before being subdued.

But the bulldogs of that time don't much resemble the bulldogs we live with now. Paintings and sketches of bulldogs from back then show a more slender dog, with longer legs and a fuller snout. Their heads were smaller and their faces were smooth. They looked more like a modern boxer than Uga. Those early bulldogs nearly went extinct when bullbaiting was outlawed in the early nineteenth century.

A quick digression: At some point in the bullbaiting era, breeders crossed bulldogs with various breeds of terrier to create a leaner, quicker dog. Some of those dogs evolved into several breeds lumped together under the category of pit bulls—dogs that have been banned in regions all over the world. Bronwen Dickey's book *Pit Bull* traces how pit bulls acquired their modern reputation mostly through human wickedness and ignorance. Some pit bull owners did (and do) train them to be vicious, and many pit bull opponents did (and do) harbor stereotypes about race and class that got transferred onto the dogs themselves. An occasional pit bull can be violent—they were bred to fight, after all. But most are as loving and lovable as any other dog.

As Dickey illustrates, the fulcrum of modern pit bull history was the arrest of star NFL quarterback Michael Vick in 2007 on several felonies related to an interstate dogfighting ring he was running on property he owned in Virginia. Vick and three friends ran the operation, and they electrocuted, drowned, or beat to death dogs that were injured or underperforming. Vick ended up serving eighteen months in federal prison and two more in home confinement before returning to football. It was one of those stories that generated outrage from several angles. Some animal lovers wanted Vick to suffer the same fate the dead dogs did. Others noted how common dogfighting is in some rural areas. Still others wondered what the big deal was—they were just pit bulls, and fighting was what pit bulls were for.

But the long tail of the story made it more interesting. Police seized fifty-one dogs in the raid on the operation, and forty-seven of them lived long enough to be adopted by families or taken in by animal rescue organizations. The dogs ended up finding homes all across the country. And as publications like *Sports Illustrated* and the *Washington Post* told those dogs' stories, it became clearer that the dogs themselves were not the problem. Pit bulls are still suspect to some people, but not as much as they used to be. And in some strange way, Michael Vick is to thank for that.

Back to regular bulldogs: As you might remember, by the middle of the nineteenth century, middle-class British families were starting to take in dogs as pets. Breeders mated the most docile bulldogs and started marketing them as a loyal companion. And along the way, they started tweaking the dog's appearance, slowly turning it into the barrel-chested drooler that so many people love. By the early twentieth century, they were cemented as one of the most popular dogs in America. Several universities besides UGA—Yale, Georgetown, Butler—adopted the bulldog as their mascot. So did the Marine Corps.

Over time, bulldogs' lives got a lot easier. They went from getting stomped by enraged bulls to snoozing on a sectional. But becoming a domestic dog—and eventually, a purebred—caused its own problems.

There have been eleven Ugas so far. All of them have been purebreds. This is a polite way of saying they're inbred.

This is not just normal in Dogland; it's standard operating procedure, although people in the fancy like to use the term "line breeding." Inbreeding, line breeding, whatever—it's the only way to create a purebred dog.

Every official AKC breed has a stud book, which is a detailed family tree of every known purebred dog of the breed. You can look up pretty much any purebred in history and trace its pedigree. At some early point in a breed's history, the stud book becomes "closed"—meaning a purebred dog can come only from dogs in the stud book. In human terms, that means the dating pool gets shallow fast. In dog terms, it means cousin mating with cousin, brother mating with sister, parent mating with child.

Dogs sometimes inbreed with one another in the wild, so it's not unnatural in that sense. But we outlaw incest among humans not just because we believe it to be criminal and immoral. We ban it because it magnifies any genetic problems a family might have. It endangers the offspring.

The problem is, people in the dog world see it the other way around. They think of inbreeding as preserving a breed's *best* traits.

Many breeders I talked to told me some version of the same thing: what matters most in the purebred world is consistency. It's crucial for both a breeder and a buyer to know what they're getting. And if the dog is a potential show dog, the stakes are even higher. The dog has to meet a breed standard carefully developed over generations. The best way to get a dog that meets the standard is to mate two dogs that already have.

Of course, that's also how genetic issues in the breed get passed down to another generation.

One reason humans are so relatively hardy, as a species, is that we pursue mates outside the family. When people from different bloodlines mate, the dominant genes of one win out over the recessive genes of the other. That matters because recessive genes cause many genetic defects and diseases. Two parents from the same family are likely to have the same recessive gene. Which means their children are likely to inherit it.

In practice, this means that nearly every breed of purebred dog has chronic health problems that never get fixed. In 2015, a group of researchers analyzed the records of nearly eighty-nine thousand dogs that came through a California veterinary hospital over a fifteen-year span. They found that purebreds were more likely than mutts to have any of ten different genetic conditions—everything from cataracts to dermatitis to bloat (a distended stomach condition that can be fatal).

It's strange, if you think about it. The forces that work so hard to keep a breed going strong make individual dogs more and more vulnerable. The price for creating a predictable dog is that they predictably die of something that might have been prevented.

Relative to other purebreds, Striker is genetically lucky. Samoyeds are generally healthy and usually live twelve to fourteen years. That's near the top end for dogs. But Samoyeds do have some known genetic flaws. They're prone to retinal diseases that can cause blindness. There's also a type of kidney failure unique to the breed, called Samoyed hereditary glomerulopathy. Dogs that get the disorder usually die by age five.

Judi Elford, Striker's breeder and co-owner, has thought a lot about what it means to constantly tweak the genetic profile of dogs. She does it all the time. She also works in a world where inbreeding is the norm. But she knows there's a natural limit once the stud book closes for good. "You can't just bottleneck your genetics," she says. "Every breed has an expiration date if you just keep breeding and breeding and breeding and nothing new comes in."

This is what's so hard to remember when you're deep inside Dogland. The number of people who care about pedigrees and breed standards is just a small neighborhood in the big city of people who own and love and care about dogs. But that small subset has literally shaped the modern dog. Somewhere deep in a bulldog's DNA is the fury and courage that could bring down a bull twenty times its size. But over the decades a mildness was bred in, along with the short muzzle and the underbite and all the problems that go along with it. You might need an electron microscope to really see it, but inside every dog is a tug-of-war between what they were and what they are, what nature wanted them to be and what humanity decided they ought to be.

The thing about it, of course, is that the dogs don't get to choose. They just have to live with the consequences.

In a tucked-away corner of Sanford Stadium, where the Georgia Bulldogs play, there is a small mausoleum. There are just nine residents, buried next to one another in a marble vault.

Each one has a marker and an epitaph:

UGA I: Damn Good Dog

UGA III: How 'bout This Dawg

UGA VI: A Big Dog for a Big Job, and He Handled It Well

Uga X has a spot waiting. (He was retired in spring 2023 and died in early 2024 at age ten.) So does the current mascot, Uga XI, and all the others to follow.

Fans stop by on game day to leave flowers or dog treats. They get their pictures taken in front of the markers. Like so many things in college football, it is a hundred percent ridiculous and a hundred percent serious at the same time. Which is why college football is the greatest sport.

If you take the broad view, every one of those bulldogs had a diamond life. They lounged in an air-conditioned doghouse. They had their own room at the on-campus hotel. They got the best food and the best care and the love of untold thousands of fans. They had it about as good as a dog ever gets.

But because of thousands of human decisions, going back hundreds of years, they also suffered. Their long-ago ancestors were sacrificed for blood sport. Their modern relatives were bred to please the eye, no matter how much it wrecked their bodies.

We have admired and adored so many dogs—the Frenchie being only the most recent—while at the same time we have caused them pain and shortened their lives.

In many ways, we have loved dogs to death.

DOGS OF MYTH AND LEGEND, RANKED

#5

Cerberus

Three-headed guard dog of the underworld in Greek mythology. Serpent for a tail. Supposedly captured by Heracles as the last of his twelve labors. "Supposedly," because there are dozens of different versions of how the capture happened. Which means even the Greek mythologists knew that defeating a three-headed dog from hell was unlikely.

#4

Gelert

Wolfhound hero in a Welsh folk tale, with variations in many cultures. In this telling, Llywelyn the Great returns home from a hunt to find chaos: his infant is missing, the cradle is overturned, and Gelert's mouth is smeared with blood. Llywelyn comes to the obvious conclusion and, in his fury, kills Gelert with his sword. Only then does he hear his baby crying. He finds the baby under the cradle, next to a dead wolf. Gelert had been protecting the child.

You might recognize a riff on this story from *Lady and the Tramp*, although Tramp survives and the wolf is replaced by a rat.

#3

Basenjis

A real dog with a strange quirk: Basenjis don't bark. They croak, or yodel, or vocalize like a British noblewoman in a 1930s comedy. The story of why they don't bark comes from the Nyanga people of central Africa. One account goes that a fire god took the Basenji's ability to speak after the dog allowed someone to steal some of the fire. Another goes that the dog silenced himself after the fire thief tried to make him the village messenger. Clearly the Basenji had workplace issues.

#2

Chinese zodiac dog

The dog is the eleventh of twelve Chinese zodiac signs named for animals. People born in the Year of the Dog are supposed to be loyal, easygoing, and sincere. They're also great at goofing off. Legend has it that the dog finished next to last in the Great Race among the zodiac animals because it stopped to play so much along the way.

#1

Argos

In book 17 of the *Odyssey*, Odysseus returns home after being away for twenty years. He is disguised as a beggar so he can sneak into his own house, which other men have taken over while he was gone. As he approaches, he sees his loyal dog. Argos had once been swift and strong. But now he is old and flea-bitten, lying on a pile of cow dung. Still, he recognizes Odysseus and wags his tail. Odysseus wipes away a tear, knowing that going to Argos would give himself away. He walks past the dog. Argos, having finally seen his master come home, dies.

And you thought *Old Yeller* was a gut punch.

6

FOR YOUR CONSIDERATION

From the minutes of the American Kennel Club's annual meeting in 1896:

Westminster Kennel Club Vs Robert Leslie.

Re: Misconduct in issuing a circular letter of attack on the W.K.C. and one of its Judges.

WHEREAS Leslie made an unjustifiable attack on one of the official Judges of the Westminster Kennel Club in a signed circular letter sent by him to the pointer breeders and exhibitors; and

WHEREAS he appeals to said pointer exhibitors to withhold their entries from the forthcoming show of the said Westminster Kennel Club, which was intended to exert an injurious effect upon the entries of a show held by a club, a member of the American Kennel Club;

it is therefore ORDERED that Robert Leslie be and is hereby suspended for a term of one year from this date.

And it is further ORDERED that this suspension shall remain in force, at the expiration of one year, until the said Leslie shall make a full apology to all parties concerned.

So, yeah, people have been complaining about the judges at dog shows for a while.

It goes back even further than that. You might remember that the event most historians think of as the first dog show happened in Newcastle, England, in 1859. There were two classes of dogs in the show: setters and pointers. The winning setter just happened to belong to the judge of the pointers. And the winning pointer just happened to belong to the judge of the setters.

There was also the show in Memphis in 1874, three years before the first Westminster. You might remember from an earlier chapter that the organizer of the show was a former Confederate soldier named P. H. Bryson. That show stands out because it was the first to give a Best in Show award. The Best in Show winner was a setter bitch named Maud, who belonged to—you are not going to believe this—P. H. Bryson.

Dog shows still tend to be incestuous, and not just among the dogs. It's a relatively small world, and there's a matrix of connections among owners and handlers and judges. But no obvious conflict of interest would fly at a modern dog show. There are safeguards in place. At Westminster in 2019, a Schipperke named Colton made it to the Best in Show round but was ruled ineligible for the title—one of his co-owners also owned dogs with the partner of Peter Green, who was the Best in Show judge that year. As connections go, it was the equivalent of being a cousin once removed. But it was enough. Colton got to take a lap around the ring at Madison Square Garden, and then he was sent home.

The conversations about judges in Dogland aren't really about corruption. They're about two main topics: tendencies and persuasion. Figuring out the first one takes a lot of time. Figuring out the second one takes a lot of money.

The key to the flow of the dog-show world is that on most weekends—major shows like Westminster excepted—there are multiple shows around the country to choose from.

Dog shows announce their roster of judges, from breed level up to Best in Show, at least five weeks before the deadline to enter the show, and often much earlier. Westminster, for example, publishes its list of judges about six months in advance. Handlers and owners have plenty of lead time to know who would judge their dogs at a particular show. And that often moves them to choose one show over another.

Serious players and coaches in every sport study the officials. Officials are supposed to be completely neutral, but the reality is they're completely human. NBA teams know how a given referee tends to behave almost as well as they know what LeBron James is likely to do at the top of the key. Some refs call a lot of traveling, and others let it go. Some refs let big guys wrestle for a spot in the paint, and others blow the whistle. Some refs unintentionally tilt the scale toward the home team, and others tend to favor the visitors.

An actual officiating scandal rocked the NBA in the

mid-2000s—ref Tim Donaghy did prison time after admitting to betting on games he refereed. But the day-to-day book on referees isn't about that. It's about natural human tendencies, how they play out over time, and how that affects the game.

Dog-show judges also have their quirks, even though they try hard not to. Some tend to favor dogs over bitches. Some favor small dogs over big ones. Some might have a favorite breed. Professional owners and handlers notice these things. An NBA coach can't do much about a ref's tendencies other than complain (and maybe get ejected for the trouble). But a dog-show handler can search future judging programs for favorable or unfavorable matchups.

A couple of years ago at the National Dog Show, I met Roxanne Sutton and her husband, Jessy. They're professional breeders and handlers from Pennsylvania. Roxanne's Norfolk terrier,* Tyler, was one of the top terriers in the country that year. They were showing *thirty-two* dogs at the National Dog Show—so many that Roxanne blanked on the name of the dog she was grooming while I was talking to her.

I asked if they were headed to the AKC National Championship in Orlando a few weeks later. I assumed they were, because most everybody else was—the AKC show is one of the American dog world's biggest events. Westminster, the National Dog Show, and the AKC are like the majors in golf and tennis.

"No Orlando," Roxanne said. They were going to the show in Allentown, Pennsylvania, instead.

---

*Norfolk terrier: British dog formerly considered the same as the Norwich terrier until The Kennel Club of the United Kingdom officially separated the breeds in 1964. The main difference: Norwich ears up, Norfolk ears down. Students at Cambridge University in the nineteenth century kept them in their dorm rooms to curb the infestation of rats.

Why?

"Because Allentown judges are so much better. A million times better. The lady that runs that show, she doesn't mess around."

Better for *you*, or just better? I asked.

She smiled.

"Better for the dogs."

Most handlers aren't quite so plainspoken about it. But they all plan their schedules based on what's better for their dogs—meaning, what gives them the best chance of ribbons and trophies and such. (The knuckleheads who gripe about participation trophies would be furious at how many ribbons a dog show gives out. There are so many that people sometimes just leave them behind at the show ring.)

All the maneuvering is based on an unspoken but accurate assumption: judging a dog show completely by the book—especially the later rounds—is basically impossible.

The breed stage is easier. There's one breed standard to remember, and it's easier to compare one similar dog with another. But at the group level, a judge is theoretically supposed to know the standards of at least twenty and as many as thirty-three breeds, depending on the group. That means being able to discern the difference between (for example) the best version of an Alaskan malamute vs. the best version of a Portuguese water dog.

The Best in Show judge has just seven dogs to choose from, but they could represent any of the AKC's two hundred breeds. Now we're talking about comparing a Pekingese with a Saint Bernard with an Afghan hound with a Dalmatian. It's like giving a chef a meal of corn on the cob, filet mignon, potato salad, and cherry pie and asking: *Which one tastes the best?* It's possible, I guess, to choose the dish that was most perfectly rendered. But it's also about what flavors you like.

There are a million theories about why some breeds and groups win more than others. Historically, terriers have won Westminster far more than any other group—forty-eight Best in Shows, or more than a third of the overall total. Wire fox terriers alone have won fifteen times. I mentioned this to David Frei, the long-time host of Westminster on TV, who now cohosts the National Dog Show. Frei has done everything in the dog world: he's been a breeder, owner, handler, and judge. He wondered if terriers tend to win because they're front-facing dogs—meaning their natural tendency is to look out ahead. Other breeds tend to look back at their handlers for support. So terriers seem more independent.

I developed a couple of theories of my own while roaming around Dogland. Theory one: smaller dogs win a lot because there's just less surface area for things to go wrong. Something as massive as a mastiff is bound to have obvious flaws. Theory two: popular breeds tend not to win because it's a subtle form of pushback to those outside the fancy. The latest *Indiana Jones* film never wins at Cannes; it's always the art flick. Golden retrievers do big at the box office, so they're doomed at the dog show.

"I think, by the time you get to Best in Show, you should have seven pretty good specimens, in terms of the individual breeds," David Frei said. "It comes down to the showmanship, if you will. Charisma. Personality."

Just to be clear: there is no science behind those theories, just observation. But observation is at the heart of not just every dog show but our normal interactions with dogs. We're all dog judges, in a way. We decide at a glance if a dog is good or bad, friendly or unfriendly, a keeper or a pass. What is somebody doing at a shelter but picking their own personal Best in Show?

This is the dilemma of every judged competition, from boxing to figure skating to *American Idol*. The outcome depends on a series of judgments from imperfect humans who might not even know their own tendencies. A different group of judges might pick a different winner. Hell, the same group of judges might pick a different winner on a different day.

It's nice to think about alternate universes where every dog gets to be Best in Show. But in our reality, every year, there's just one winner.

And so the professionals in Dogland do their damnedest to make sure the judges know their dogs before they ever meet in the ring.

When Westminster was at Madison Square Garden, the best free show in town was in the hotel lobbies around the arena. The first year I went, in 2020, I booked a room at the New Yorker Hotel—one of the two main Westminster hotels back then, along with the Hotel Pennsylvania. The lobby at the New Yorker was packed with dogs lounging on the floor and slinking onto the ancient elevators and barking somewhere high above. The dogs were the first thing that caught my eye. The second was the stacks of magazines on every available flat space. *Dog News. The Canine Chronicle. Showsight.* They're the big trade magazines for the dog-show world. Their Westminster editions are the size of a graphic novel. There were also magazines for several of the most popular breeds. Print still thrives at dog shows. And all the magazines have one thing in common: glamour shots that are so beautifully and lushly rendered that they come close to doggy porn.

To give you a sense, I just now pulled one issue from the stack on my bookshelf—a copy of *Dog News* from October 2021. There's a helpful guide in the back with the ad rates: $1,500 for page 3, $1,700 for a double spread on pages 20 and 21, $900 for page 31 if you're on a budget. They are doing a booming business. Twenty-three of the first thirty-five pages are ads.

There are three basic motifs. One is a still life of dog and handler, looking thoughtfully at the camera. The second is the same pair in action, midtrot around the show ring. The third is the money shot. It's the dog and handler posing with a trophy or ribbon—and usually with the judge who awarded it.

"Thank you to the Judges," says an ad for a beagle named Jack. "Thank You Judge," in three different places, says an ad for a Great Pyrenees named Sebastian. A two-page ad for a Lakeland terrier named Flash features four different photos with four different judges, plus a shout-out to a fifth judge in a graphic.

They're the Dogland version of those "For Your Consideration" ads that show up in the Hollywood trades at awards time. Beautifully photographed star. List of other recent awards. A nudge to the voter who might not be completely informed about all the candidates. The only difference is that the campaign is centered around a German shepherd instead of Nicolas Cage. (Although Nicolas Cage would totally play a German shepherd if the price was right.)

There's no money changing hands here, except between the dogs' owners and the publications. But the message isn't subtle, either. *Look at this creature! Isn't it glorious? Other judges thought this dog was just great. When the time comes, YOU should think the same thing.*

Pages 8 and 9 of this very issue ($1,950) feature Laura King and Striker. One photo is Striker holding his stack at the Morris & Essex show as a judge in a feathered hat strolls by. The second is Laura and Striker in motion, Laura with a black dress and a great giddy expression, Striker in midstride with all four feet off the ground. Above and to the left is the word "Striker" in big stylized letters with a flame dotting the *i*. They drop in a couple of hashtags for social media: #WHITENOISE and #NOSMILENOSAMMY. They make sure to thank the judge.

Every word, every image, every font is designed to be memorable. It's not exactly subliminal advertising. It is meant to plant a thought in a judge's mind, conscious or not.

"There are judges who are less comfortable because they might be newer," Laura told me. "If you came from Scottish terriers and now you're judging Samoyeds, it's a completely different look. You probably haven't spent your entire lifetime looking at those breeds. You pick up a magazine and you see, 'Oh, look at this dog.' It's won ninety-three Best in Shows and whatever—it must be a pretty good dog. Then if you have it in the ring and you're like, 'Well, I don't know what to do here' . . . this one has won ninety-three Best in Shows."

Laura explained how a normal campaign for a promising show dog usually works. In year one she would pick ten or twelve shows where the dog would be most likely to have a friendly judge to "get some buzz going." They'd build a series of ads off any big wins from that year. Year two would involve a bigger variety of shows, in front of a cross-section of judges, to find out whether the dog has a broader appeal. The goal there is to rack up some wins that can be featured in the next round of ads. Then year three would be full blast—a full slate of shows with the long game of winning big at Westminster or one of the other majors.

Striker didn't take that path. His owners showed him in Canada first, and he won a bunch of shows up there before they decided to give him a shot in the States. Then Laura's first year with him ended up being 2020, the year that COVID hit, which meant they did no shows for months. Those first post-COVID shows were only in states that relaxed their guidelines early, such as Florida, which usually meant there was only one show on a given weekend. So judge shopping went out the window.

In a way, though, the restrictions proved Striker's strength. He won no matter the judge and no matter the size of the field. Laura came out of it convinced that Striker was good enough to win Best in Show anywhere.

That meant his owners would be getting out their checkbooks.

Striker's owners are two Canadian couples. One couple is Judi and Blair Elford—you might remember Judi Elford as one of Striker's breeders, the one who picked him from the litter and gave him his name. The other couple are longtime friends of theirs, Correen Pacht and Marc Ralsky. Correen's background is in real estate and Marc is a fundraiser for nonprofits.

Marc and Correen had specialized in Siberian huskies. But they had heard Judi talk about Striker, so they went to Orlando in 2018 to watch Judi show him there. He won the Working Group.

Marc and Correen fell in love with him. They agreed to pool their resources with the Elfords to see how far Striker could go.

Nobody in Dogland likes to talk about money—at least not directly. When I asked how much it costs to run a full campaign for a top show dog, everybody hedged and fudged. But it was clear that it runs at least in the low six figures. Laura mentioned once in passing about owners spending $400,000 a year. Other handlers mentioned $200,000. Somewhere between a ranch house and a Bentley.

Daybreak Kennel, Laura and Robin's business, lists basic costs on their website: $110 per dog per show as a handling fee, $50 an hour for conditioning, $15 to $18 a day for boarding. Plus bonuses if the dog wins its group or Best in Show and so forth. Plus a share of gas and mileage to keep Betty White on the road. It adds up fast even if you hire Laura for just a weekend. Striker has lived with her for nearly three years.

And none of that counts the ads in the trade magazines, the photographers to shoot those ads, or the graphic designers to make them look pretty.

The very best dogs, like Striker, will make some money for their owners through stud fees. But it doesn't begin to cover the costs of owning a top show dog. It doesn't make any sense if you think of it as a business proposition. Which is why almost nobody in Dogland thinks of it as a business proposition.

Marc and Correen are Canadian, so they frame it in terms of hockey. What if they had kids who played on a travel team? How much would it cost to buy all their equipment, pay for training, and drive them from here to Halifax and back?

"It's a hobby," Marc said in one of our conversations. "And if you're playing at a certain level, you put more money into it, because you have to."

"Right," Correen said.

"And so we did," Marc said.

Other owners told me versions of the same thing. And at first, it sounded phony to me. Surely these folks were making some backdoor money that I just couldn't see. Surely they weren't spending hundreds of thousands of dollars a year just to prove that their Yorkshire terrier was better than everybody else's Yorkshire terrier.

But then I thought about all the other obsessives I've met over the years. The NASCAR fans who show up in their RVs on Monday when the main race isn't until Sunday. The surfers who fly halfway across the world at the rumor of big waves. Not all those folks spend as much as the owner of a top show dog does, but some do. Chances are they don't dwell on it much. An obsession only seems excessive if it's not *your* obsession.

A dog handler named Betty Feezor told me something early on that helped me understand Dogland as much as anything I'd learned along the way. Don't think of the dog as an investment, she said. Think of it like a piece of art. The owner might never get out of it what they put into it. But they own that particular piece of art. No one else does. And they get to show it off.

Judi Elford thinks of it as the place where art meets science. The science is breeding and genetics. The art is the product of the science, and the science serves the art. One afternoon she started talking about crossbreeds like Labradoodles, then moved to how all the Samoyeds in existence came from just a dozen dogs one hundred years ago, then to the difference between dogs created to do important work and the dogs created to look cute. After a while she shrugged. Maybe we were both overthinking this.

"I haven't had five bored minutes at a dog show in my life," she says. "It rings my bells."

Now Striker is under the lights in the Westminster ring, about to compete in the Working Group, and Judi is in Spain. They are having the World Dog Show in Madrid, and Judi had booked the trip months before, expecting Westminster 2022 to move back to its normal time slot in February. But Westminster decided to keep its place in June. Judi promised a friend they could meet in Madrid. So she is up in her hotel at three in the morning, watching the livestream, as the dogs and handlers head down the artificial turf ramp lined on both sides with lights, like the aisle of a plane.

The FOX Sports announcers set the scene. "The group winner from last year is back," says Gail Miller Bisher. "Striker the Samoyed."

It takes him a while to come out. There are thirty-one dogs in the Working Group, and alphabetically, the Samoyed is fourth from the end. Laura has Striker on a lead in her left hand and gear to keep him comfortable in her right: spray bottle, portable fan, towel. At every show Laura and her crew designate one of their many towels as Striker's lucky towel for that show. This time around it's a blue one. His comb is under the rubber band that holds her armband in place. Each dog has a spot on the arena floor, marked by a yellow box with its breed name. There's a huge spray of flowers in between every fourth box. The judge, Faye Strauss, is wearing a black evening gown. This ain't the Greater Hickory Kennel Club.

But up in the crowd, the culture clash is fascinating. There's a guy in a polo and khakis who looks like he just stepped off a yacht. There's a woman in an American-flag denim jacket who looks like she just dismounted a Harley. Somebody brought in two pizzas from outside. The storied Lyndhurst estate feels a little like Madison Square Garden after all.

Outside it's misting rain. In here it's cold to counteract the heat of the TV lights. There's a buzz in the crowd. In the ring, there is a lot of waiting as the judge looks at each dog one by one. Laura kneels and scratches Striker's jaw. Striker occasionally notices the dogs as they trot past him. But he spends most of his time scanning the crowd or watching his shadow or looking at the judges and VIPs coming through the door that says BLACK TIE ENTRANCE.

Each dog, on its own, is beautiful. Collectively, being inspected one by one, it can be a little tedious for the fans. But around the time the Boerboel* named Leo takes his turn, something interesting happens. A pitiful howl rises up from somewhere in the ring.

None of us in the press area can pinpoint where it's coming from. The TV announcers ignore it at first. But by the third or fourth moan, with the crowd laughing and chattering, they have to say something. Somebody identifies the howler: the Alaskan malamute, Tyce. He's been in front of the judge already. Maybe he's bored. Maybe he's hungry. Maybe he is having a moment

---

*Boerboel: Huge (150–200 pound) mastiff-bulldog breed developed in South Africa by white European settlers in the 1600s. Fearless protector also used to hunt everything from baboons to lions. Banned in several countries because of fears of aggressiveness.

of existential crisis, wondering how and why he was born to be a sled dog, chugging across the tundra, but somehow wound up combed and spritzed and led around a fake grass rug in a TV tent.

Probably he's just bored.

Whatever the reason, it's like a cold spray of reality. All these dogs are so, so quiet. Way back at the beginning of the book I mentioned how curious it was that the dogs don't bark. But to be honest, by this point, after three years of dog shows, I was used to it. Silence was their default mode. But we all know that's not how it usually works.

At least twenty years ago, when I was working on a writing seminar about using short words, I came up with a list of dog verbs. Almost everything a dog does can be described in one-syllable words: drool, lick, jump, stretch, fetch, gnaw, chase, wag. And a lot of dog verbs describe their sounds: bark, howl, yip, growl, slurp, pant, yawn, moan.

Dogs are supposed to bark and yip and moan. It's part of how we define a dog.

Tyce was a reminder that Dogland is like Disney World: so charming and pleasant that you forget it's not quite real. It was as if Mickey Mouse took off his head and the guy in the suit started talking. I could see a couple of the dog show officials on the sideline looking flustered as Tyce kept singing into the ether. But to me this made the show even better. Those were real dogs out there. They drool and fart and lick their crotches. Their human partners were just as normal, just as frail and flawed. But together they created an illusion of control. They were so good at it that one howl made me marvel at all the howls that did not happen. They were just dogs, and it was just a dog show, but it felt like something extraordinary.

Michael LaFave's voice: "Originating in Siberia, the Samoyed is the utility dog of the North. This breed is willing to do any job asked of them . . ."

The judge approaches Striker. Checks his bite, his chest, his ribs, his haunches, his balls. She asks Laura to do a "down and back"—a quick straight-line trot out into the ring, then back to the judge. Laura pulls Striker in a tight circle to get him ready. He seems unfocused. He does a long shake, as if he has just come out of the pool. Laura slides her hand down on the lead until there are just a couple of inches between them. She doesn't look at him. She just holds still. He glances up at her. He holds still.

Then they take off and he is gliding.

"Loud roar from this crowd," says FOX Sports host Chris Myers.

"He has a following," says Gail Miller Bisher.

In the background, Tyce howls in approval. Or despair. Or something.

The rest of the dogs get their turns, and all the handlers rise and get their dogs into the stack position. The judge does one more walkthrough, smiling at thirty-one handlers, thirty of whom will soon be disappointed.

Most judges at this point make a first cut of eight to ten dogs before picking the winner. Some judges cull as few as six. Strauss goes through, pointing at dogs in alphabetical order. The Cane

Corso. The Doberman. The giant schnauzer. The Kuvasz. The Leonberger. The Portuguese water dog.

Striker is her seventh pick.

She adds the standard schnauzer and lines up the eight dogs in order.

"This is the hard part," Bisher says.

Striker is excited all of a sudden. He runs in a circle, makes Laura whirl around.

The judge sends them all on one last lap around the ring. She lines them up, takes them in all at once, spreads her arms wide.

"A great group of dogs," she says.

She pauses.

Looks at Laura.

"Could you pull your dog out right over here?" she says.

In Madrid, at three in the morning, Judi Elford screams so loud she wakes up her friend.

For the second year in a row, Striker has beaten out some two thousand dogs to make it to the final round at Westminster. Most dogs never get there once.

He has also delayed his retirement for a couple more hours. One more at-bat, and he gets to take it in game seven of the World Series.

Does he know? Does he care? Who knows? Laura cares. Judi and Blair care. Marc and Correen care. They bred and trained and loved their dog, and they got him to the final level of Dogland.

Jamie Little, the Westminster sideline reporter, interviews Laura. She and Striker are standing on a rug decorated with an outline of Sensation, Westminster's ideal dog. For the moment, he is under their feet.

"How do you do this two years in a row, Laura?" Jamie Little says.

"I don't know. I have no idea. Ask someone else. It's incredible."

She's being modest for the camera. She knows exactly how it is done.

Someone leads the dogs and handlers that did not win down a corridor and around a corner, and all of a sudden they're outside. It could not be a clearer signal that their Westminster is over. Two security guards are marveling at the Neapolitan mastiff, a charcoal-colored giant with the build of a fullback and the face of a thousand-year-old man. The spot outside the tent is where the dogs and handlers reunite with their families and teams. Every dog out here right now not only is a finished champion but won their breed at the most important dog show in the country. But the air is full of disappointment. There is a lot of shrugging, out here in the cold damp evening, and also a few tears. A handler leans on a railing near the steps and steals a smoke.

Inside, Laura kneels beside Striker as they pose for photos as winners of the Working Group. There are a bunch of photographers lined up behind a velvet rope, and Striker keeps looking away from the cameras. He doesn't appear to be upset by the clicks and flashes. He just doesn't seem to care. Sam Hanle, one of Laura and Robin's assistants, finally steps into the middle of the row of photogs. She shows Striker a treat. Pure bribery. It works.

I'm lined up with Laura and Striker but off to the side, out of photo range. From this vantage point I can see the depth of Striker, the curve of his chest, the fullness of his coat, the length of his snout as it feeds back to his coal-black eyes. My wife, Alix, looked over my shoulder one time as I was scrolling through pictures of Striker and said: "It's so funny. He looks two-dimensional." Now it's all I see when I look at photos of him. She's right. The people around him look like they're in 3D, and so do most of the dogs, but Striker looks somehow pasted in. Maybe it's because he's so utterly black and white in a world of color. Maybe it's because his fur is so bright it's hard to distinguish his features. You always hear about how supermodels and actors aren't as dazzling in person. Striker is the opposite. Up close he's substantial in a way photos don't capture. It's easy to see why so many people have invested so much in him.

"Just a few more," one of the photographers says, and Laura and Striker lean into each other.

The photogs leave and Laura stands up, and it's not clear what to do next. A steward comes by and says they need to go to the ready room. Laura takes Striker and they head down the corridor where the other dogs went a few minutes before.

"No," the steward says. "That's outside. You don't have to go outside."

She points them the right way. For a little while longer, Laura and Striker are still in the tent.

Interlude

A STRAY

We will get back to Striker and Laura in a little bit, I promise. But you probably know that if you talk to a dog person, eventually you're going to hear about their dog. So here is the story of our dog.

I went out to get the paper one fall morning in 2001. My wife and I were living in the first house we bought together, a ranch house with a big yard north of uptown Charlotte. It had a long driveway. When I got to the end, I saw something wriggling in the ditch. A puppy the color of beach sand. His tail wagged so hard when I picked him up.

My wife was still asleep, so I brought him to her. *Alix*, I whispered. *Look*. She can barely see without her glasses. We had a cat back then, a tabby named Rocket, and she was puzzled as to why I was showing her the cat. Then she put on her glasses. She saw two things I had not noticed: the puppy's belly was bloated, and he was crawling with fleas. *Let's get him out of the house*, she said.

We took him to the garage. We gave him some cat food and he scarfed it down. We stared at him and then at each other. Neither of us was sure what to do next. Our neighbors Bill and Susie had a fenced-in yard, so I took him over there to give us some time to figure it out. As I walked back across the street, I looked down, and he was right on my heels. He had squeezed through the gate and followed me home.

It was just a few weeks after the 9/11 attacks. Like a lot of people, we were still staggering. We had a hole in our lives that we had no idea how to fill. Fate brought us a dog.

I wanted to name him Herschel, after the legendary University of Georgia tailback Herschel Walker. Alix, who is from Wisconsin and did not grow up on SEC football, vetoed that one. (Given Herschel's later political career, this was a good call.) We tried on other names but none quite fit. Then I thought about a scene from one of my favorite movies from college, *The Sure Thing*, a rom-com starring John Cusack and Daphne Zuniga. They play bickering college students hitchhiking across the country who slowly realize they're falling in love. On one of their rides, Zuniga's character daydreams about finding a husband and having a baby. If they had a boy, she says, she'd name him Elliott. Cusack objects. "Nick," he says. "Nick's your buddy. Nick's . . . the kinda guy you can drink a beer with. The kinda guy that doesn't mind if you puke in his car. Nick."

Somehow this dog didn't look like a Nick. But he did look like he could be our buddy.

How about Fred? I said. *You can trust a Fred.*

So he was Fred.

Our free dog cost us a couple hundred dollars right off for shots at the vet and flea medicine and neutering. Then he cost us a couple thousand dollars for a new fence in the backyard. Before we could get the fence built, he ate most of our garage. He chewed up the attachments for the Shop-Vac. He gnawed on the drywall. Under our workbench, we kept a twenty-foot-long plumbing snake coiled up in a five-gallon bucket. One day I came home from work to find the snake unspooled on the garage floor. Fred had eaten the top of the bucket until the snake popped out. If it had scared him, he'd gotten over it—by the time we got there, he was wagging like crazy, showing off what he'd done. Then he shat white plastic for a week.

Fred was not a show dog. He was a mutt. He seemed to be mostly yellow Lab, but slimmer, especially toward the back end. The vet thought he might have some German shorthaired pointer in him. His fur had a few darker spots, including one on his forehead, like a bindi dot. The vet guessed he was a couple months old when he showed up at our house. We never learned where he came from. We asked around the neighborhood to find out if anyone had lost a puppy, but to be honest we didn't try very hard. We fell in love fast.

Our cat, Rocket, taught him as much as we did. The first time they met, Fred backed him into a corner—just trying to play—until Rocket froze him with two left hooks to the nose. Later on, we picked up pecans one morning from the trees in our backyard while Fred and Rocket played around us. Rocket would bait Fred into chasing him, and just when Fred got close, he'd scamper up a tree. Fred would wait at the bottom for a minute or two, then get bored and come back over to us. The moment that happened, Rocket zipped down and sauntered into Fred's line of sight. Fred would jump in place, like in a cartoon, and take off after Rocket—who would then go right back up the tree. Rinse, repeat. Fifteen yards for taunting.

Around that time we took Fred down to Georgia to see my family. My sister and brother-in-law, Brenda and Ed, had a black Lab named Betsy in a fenced-in yard, so Fred stayed with them. Every morning Ed would pour Betsy's dog food for the day in a big bowl in the yard. The first morning Fred was there, he ran over and planted his feet on both sides of the bowl and ate every nugget. The next day, too. We somehow didn't piece together that he was eating *all* the food, and when we went to take him home, he was nearly as big around as he was long. We put him in the back seat and he moaned all the way home.

Like most dogs, Fred decided pretty much anything could be food. We had a pond next to the house, and Canada geese spent a lot of time there. Fred decided their turds were delicious. We would try to steer him clear when we went on walks, but his nose was like a dowsing rod for those damn things. He never seemed all that interested in other animal poop. Maybe the goose turds were the perfect size and shape. Tootsie Rolls for dogs.

One Sunday morning, Fred got into a box of bathroom supplies—we were getting the room redone and had boxed up the stuff we had in there. While we dressed for church, Fred found, and ate, a bar of soap. The closest vet open on a Sunday morning was a PetSmart half an hour away. I did a quick Google search on "dog eating soap." The results ranged from "it'll be fine" to "oh God, the dog is gonna die." Never Google when you're stressed.

We raced him to the vet and then sat in the waiting room for two hours. We watched for signs of distress, but he just curled up on the floor. Finally we got in to see the vet. He said he could give Fred something to make him throw up, but if he hadn't had a reaction by now, he'd probably be fine. The vet also told us that, sometimes, dogs that ate soap would fart bubbles. We followed him around with a camera for hours. Not a single fart bubble. He owed us a damn fart bubble.

Fred was an orphan, and we tried to imagine what the first few weeks of his life were like, before he found us. He startled easily. For a while he would camp out under our coffee table, but anytime there was a sudden movement, he'd leap up and bonk his head on the underside. We suspected he got a couple of dog concussions. But he was also scared of odd, specific things. He cowered from white vans. He was terrified of children—not just children, but stuff that was child-adjacent. One morning when we were out on a walk, he circled way out into the street to avoid a Big Wheel some kid had left on the sidewalk. We pieced together a dark story in our heads about mean children and white vans. We wished he could tell us what had happened to him so we could keep him safe.

Like a lot of dogs, he could not handle thunder or fireworks. Even when he was full-grown and sixty-five pounds, at the first clap of thunder he would run over to me or Alix and jam himself between the backs of our legs and the couch. We would laugh at this big dog with his head wedged underneath us and his ass sticking out, exposed to God's explosions. But there was real terror in his eyes.

We have all these Fred stories, stories we still tell, but some days what I remember are the in-between times, when he slowly changed from this odd new presence to this creature we had to take care of to a member of the family. The times when he stopped us on our walks because he decided he had been a good boy and it was time for a treat. The times when he skittered across the tile floor of the pet store after he got his nails clipped. The times when we put him in the back seat for a road trip and he would clamber up between us, put his front feet on the console, and rest his chin on my shoulder while I drove.

I mentioned the Canada geese. They would often waddle into our yard and crap on every square foot of grass and concrete. One day, after an especially merciless carpet-bombing, Alix spent hours hosing down our driveway, our carport, and the walkway to the house. The next morning she looked out the window and saw them back in the same spot. She decided to literally release the hound. Fred was still young enough to be sleeping in the garage. The geese were right outside the garage door. Alix hit the opener and Fred shot through the gap. It took another few seconds for the door to open enough for Alix to get out. Her plan worked—the geese were skittering across the yard toward the pond. But there was something she hadn't noticed when she looked out the window: the geese had brought their chicks with them. And now Fred had one in his mouth.

Alix ran after him, mortified. Fred thought this was a great game and went tearing around the yard as she chased him. After a minute Alix had an idea. She ran back in the garage and grabbed a dog treat. She came out and showed it to him, and he immediately ran over and dropped the chick. It wasn't hurt, although it now had one hell of a story. It went running off toward its flock. Fred had held that chick in his mouth for two or three minutes and never bit down.

Sometimes, when we roughhoused, he would open his jaw and flash his fearsome teeth and clamp down on my arm, but so softly he wouldn't have cracked an egg. I often think about how many thousands of generations of dog it took to produce a sixty-five-pound slab of muscle that never once bit anything in anger. We'll never know if it was breeding or luck. But we were blessed with such a gentle dog.

That house with the pond had a huge backyard—almost as deep as a football field and wooded around the edges. In the mornings I'd let Fred roam back there without a leash. I'd lean on a post at the corner of our garden fence as he poked around the perimeter, trotting through the dew, sniffing anything new and strange. After ten or fifteen minutes, I'd whistle as loud as I could. Way back in the corner of the lot, he'd swivel around to look. I'd hold up the treat I'd stashed in my pocket. And then he would take off running.

I always assumed this was the best moment of his day. They were some of the best moments of my life.

Every mutt is built from spare parts, and Fred had sort of a cockeyed gait. His back legs would veer off to one side. He was never exactly graceful. Except when he ran. In those early mornings he'd hit full speed in three strides, and all those pieces from whatever he was would lock into place, as if this particular sprint was what he had always been bred to do. He would come flying down the straightaway along the garden fence and start to slam on the brakes, but he always zoomed right past me, kicking up clods of grass. Then he'd hustle back to get his treat. He would be panting and wagging and slobbering, a dog in full. I'm not one of those "I would give anything to . . ." people. But damn. I would give almost anything to watch him run again.

Every so often, when he saw a chance, he'd go on a walkabout. Sometimes we'd forget to latch the gate to the dog pen, or sometimes I'd get lax at the end of the day and leave him off the leash between the pen and the house. By the time I knew what was going on, he'd be halfway down the street. This was when he did the one thing that would reliably piss me off: every time I got close to him, he'd trot just out of my reach. He'd even look over his shoulder to rub it in. Only now do I realize he probably learned this trick from Rocket.

Once, when we had friends in from out of town, he decided that was a good time to go inspect our neighbors' backyards. I was steaming by the time I caught up to him. I had forgotten to bring a leash, so I just picked him up and hauled him back home, cursing in his ear the whole way. I'm ashamed now to think about the times I yelled at him, or yanked on his leash when he pulled, or thumped him in the ribs when he was eating yet another piece of trash off the ground. Sometimes you can bond with a dog so tight that you think it understands your every thought and acts to meet your desires. It's a shock when the dog defies you. *Don't you know not to run off? Haven't we told you not to do that?* Somehow it's worse when a dog does it. We expect people to disappoint us at some point. We expect dogs to please us forever. We forget what the dog wants. Dogs wander. Dogs chafe at the leash. No matter how big a dog run they have, they always wear out a path around the edge. They always want to see more.

Two and a half years after Fred showed up, we decided to move. We loved the big yard and the garden, but it had gotten to be too much for Alix and me to take care of. We looked at houses for months. Correction: Alix looked at houses for months while I was on the road for work. Back then I was writing a column for the *Charlotte Observer*, and the Carolina Panthers were in the NFL playoffs, so the paper sent me along. The Panthers ended up making it all the way to the Super Bowl. For a month or so I'd be gone for a few days and then come back to look at a bunch of new houses Alix had picked out. Some of them I hated from the moment I walked in the door. Others had some fatal flaw. There was a neighborhood called Plaza Midwood that we both loved—it had some of the few remaining old houses in Charlotte, and at the time they were still affordable. We looked at house after house, but none was ever quite right. I told Alix we should give up on Plaza Midwood. The very next day, she was driving through and saw a FOR SALE sign in front of a house we hadn't looked at. Of course that turned out to be the one.

Fred's life changed along with ours. Our new backyard was about the size of his old dog run, but now it was surrounded by city life—a parade of neighbors on the sidewalk, the white noise of traffic on busy streets. There was no morning sprint anymore. We took him on walks, and he seemed to enjoy them, but he was always leashed up. He didn't bark a lot, but sometimes when I was working inside, I'd hear him hollering. I wondered if he was reminding us he was back there alone.

We brought him in at night, and at bedtime I'd let him into the backyard to pee. Some nights he decided he wanted to reinspect the same place he had spent most of the day. I'd stand on our tiny deck at the top of the stairs, begging him in a stage whisper to come back in. He'd look at me and poke his nose back in the bushes. It never lasted that long. Maybe he just wanted me to come down and play.

He slept in a crate in our mudroom for a long time, first with the door closed, then with it open. But before too long he wanted to be closer to us. Somewhere, generations ago, his kind had been trained not to jump on things. The whole time we had him, he never once got on the bed or our couch or the kitchen counter. We put a dog bed in the corner of the bedroom and he curled up there.

Every morning at seven, if we weren't up yet, he would come over and shove the side of the bed with his shoulder. If we didn't react right off, he would work his way around all three sides, pushing over and over until one of us caved and got up. Some nights, Alix and I would lie there in the dark and talk about some problem we were trying to work out, some funny thing that happened at work—anything, really, just the soft drowsy chatter of love. After a while, Fred would draw in a deep breath and let out a long exaggerated sigh. *Would you people shut up already*. Even if we were talking about something serious, it always cracked us up. He was our alarm clock in reverse.

He watched us close, learned our body language. One weekend Virgil, my best friend, came to visit. Fred was outside when Virgil came in, so when I let Fred in, Virgil was already on the couch. Fred was wary of strangers, so he positioned himself in the next room while Virgil and I talked about what we always talked about—old Warner Bros. cartoons or Mel Brooks movies or Richard Pryor bits. Fred had been watching us for a good hour by the time Alix got home. She came in and hugged Virgil, and when she did that, Fred trotted right over to him. Apparently the touch was the signal. He said hello by planting his nose in Virgil's crotch.

Sometimes, when I watched a ball game on TV, I'd jump out of the chair and pump my fist if something good happened. Fred would dash over from his dog bed and snuggle up close, rubbing his snout against my leg, like he was trying to give me comfort. To be fair, when you're a sports fan, joy and anguish can look the same. I would bend down and rub his ears and try to explain that it was fine. It reminded me that there would always be a gap between us. Things we would never understand about each other, no matter how close we got.

He dreamed, or at least we assumed he was dreaming. He'd be lying asleep on his side, and all of a sudden his legs would start pumping in a pantomime of running. Alix and I called it "chasing rabbits." He'd chase rabbits for a minute or two, and then his legs would stop and his breathing would slow down and he'd lay quiet again. Scientists are pretty sure dogs dream. Their brain waves in those moments are similar to ours when we're dreaming. But what do dogs dream of? What did Fred dream of? What was he chasing, or running from? I would have given an awful lot for the answer.

Fred was an introvert. If we had to fly somewhere, we dropped him off at a kennel called Pet Paradise. There was a courtyard in the middle where the dogs could play together—it even had a little swimming pool shaped like a bone. Fred was a rare Lab that didn't like water. He didn't like scrabbling around with the other dogs, either. He would stand around for a while and go back to his own little space.

When we took him on walks and ran into other dogs, sometimes he would sniff their butts. It's always OK to sniff another dog's butt. That's dog law. But just as often he would hang back, not acting scared, just watching quietly. We wondered if he got separated from his mother too soon to learn how to act around other dogs. One time we took him to a dog park with a couple of acres inside a chain-link fence. There was a group of dogs roaming around together when we came in. The moment we took Fred off the leash and he jogged that way, they jumped him. I'll never know if it was playful or mean, whether it was normal dog roughhousing or some sort of gang initiation. Whatever it was, he yelped and ran to the far end of the dog park. He stood there by himself, looking at the rest of the dogs, then went off sniffing at the base of the fence. I stood there in the middle and started to cry. I'd always felt like a loner myself. My mom had two children from her first marriage, but they were much older, and I was the only child of my mom and dad's marriage. I spent a lot of time playing by myself growing up, scoring incredible imaginary touchdowns where I was both the quarterback and the receiver. Even though I was always a big kid, I still got bullied sometimes. That was one moment when I felt like I knew exactly what Fred was feeling. We let him roam a little longer, until all of us calmed down, then we scooped him up and took him home.

He loved car rides. He was never one of those dogs that tore up the seats or tried to jump out the window. We would put an old fitted sheet over the back seat of my green Camry, and he was always ready to go. That turned out to be the solution when he got away and went on one of his walkabouts. We finally figured out, one of those times, to double back and get the car. No matter how determined he had been to run away, as soon as he saw the open car door, he jumped right in. The back windows went just halfway down, and he'd prop his chin on the edge and drool on the glass and let the breeze fill his snout. If it was a long drive, he'd settle in and sleep most of the way.

As he got older and became more of an indoor dog, it made things complicated when we went to see my mom or Alix's folks. (My dad passed long ago.) I don't think any of them really liked dogs. My mom had been bitten as a little girl and was scared of dogs in general. None of them were used to having a dog in the house. There were some tight smiles when Fred came trotting onto the clean carpet. But Fred had his own anxieties. At my mom's, he had to go through the kitchen to get to the spare bedroom we used. He wanted to go under the kitchen table, maybe because it felt safer, but there was an air vent under there. Fred was terrified of air vents. The only thing we could figure was that he thought there was a beast under the house, breathing. So he would start under the table until he got to the vent, then back out and go around and decide he didn't like that, either—maybe it was the hum of the refrigerator?—and so he'd just stand there awhile, feinting one way or the other, until he finally mustered the courage to pick a path and go.

My mom tolerated Fred for the first few years, even though she made it clear that dogs belonged outside. She didn't want him rubbing up on her or licking her fingers. After a while he figured it out and kept his distance. One day Alix and I left him with her and went out for something. When we came back, she had figured out how to get him through the kitchen. She just made a trail out of little pieces of bacon on the floor. My mom believed that most problems could be solved by pork products. So she'd make sure to cook up some bacon for Fred whenever we came to visit. It was on one of those visits, as she led him on his bacon trail, that she looked at him and said:

He's getting old.

You've probably heard the formula that one dog year equals seven human years. The science doesn't bear that out. Dogs grow up fast and then the years smooth out. There's no exact way to figure it, but the American Veterinary Medical Association breaks it down like this: the first year of a dog is equal to fifteen human years, the second year is nine, and every year after that is five.

Sometime in 2015, Fred turned fourteen years old. In human years, he was eighty-four.

It's hard to get a true perspective on aging if you're too close to it. It's like a shoreline eroding. If you go there every day, you don't even notice. If you go there once a year, it's all you can see.

We knew his hips had gone bad. Our neighbor down the street started calling him the Little Soldier because his back legs goose-stepped when he walked. He had that same odd ritual lots of dogs have where he circled a spot five or six times before he sat down. But now he circled one way, then another, then maybe back the first way, delaying as long as possible that moment when his hips hit the ground. Sometimes he would come over and lean into me hard as I rubbed his hip joints. There wasn't much muscle back there anymore.

We had made him an indoor dog when he started falling on the flight of steps down to the backyard. If he was coming up the steps, no big deal—he'd just get back to his feet. But going downhill, he'd lose control and end up in a baffled heap on the ground. It never seemed to hurt him that much, but for me it was a punch to the heart. It didn't take long for us to bring him inside for good.

There are just two short steps from our front porch to the front yard. As his hips got worse, he started having a hard time with those. We bought one of those harnesses with a handle on top so we could haul him up and down the steps like a suitcase. Then he had trouble just standing up. We'd roust him for a trip outside and notice that he'd wet the dog bed. Once he got moving, he'd be OK for a while. I used to love taking him for his midnight pee. I'd look at the stars or listen to the leaves while he inspected the bushes and fire hydrant out front, checking his pee-mail. But it wasn't long before outside didn't interest him that much anymore. He'd do his business as soon as he got to open grass and then turn back around for the house.

I'd like to say we were on top of this in the moment and understood what was happening. But the truth is that we were just living day by day, and each tiny turn of the dial was hard to see. I suspect there was also some denial in there. We still had young Fred in our minds and hearts. We superimposed that image over the dog in front of us.

That September, Alix took Fred to see her parents while I was on the road for work. When she got back home, she noticed a few drops of blood on the sheet she had draped over the back seat for him. When they got inside, he sneezed and sprayed blood all over the floor.

We took him to see our vet, Dr. Mary Fluke. She had treated Fred since he was a puppy. We loved and trusted her. She hadn't seen him for a few months, and she remarked how much he had gone downhill. She couldn't tell why he had bled, so she set him up with a specialist. In the meantime, she said, we ought to start thinking about the end. At his age and in his shape, any time would be the right time.

We took him to the specialist. They found a big tumor on his liver. They couldn't tell if it was cancer. The only way to know would be to take it out. The surgery would probably kill him.

This, of course, is the unspoken contract of having a pet. The natural order of things is that you will die before your child. Pets reverse the order. When we decided to keep that wriggling puppy we found in the ditch, we sentenced ourselves to this moment.

Maybe this is why we connect so deeply with dogs. We spend every penny of joy before the bill comes due.

Alix and I cried about it, but there wasn't much of a decision to be made. We said no to the surgery. We told Dr. Fluke. She said to let her know when we were ready.

We tried to make the last weeks special, as much for us as for him. We fed him tuna and bacon. We took him for rides every day. He didn't want to walk much, but one day he tugged me down the block to the stand where a neighbor leaves out a dish of water and a jar of dog treats. For years it was one of Fred's favorite places. He hadn't been there for months. That's when I started to believe he knew.

We told him stories about his exploits: that time he found a snapping turtle in his dog pen, that time we went outside late one night and saw a deer calmly standing in the yard next door. I reminded him of what I believe to be the greatest moment of his life: when I was grilling burgers and dropped one on the ground and let him eat it. Did he remember any of it? Who knows? We remember it all.

On one of his last nights, I took him out for his late pee, and when he was done, I sat with him on the top step of the porch. Alix came out to join us. He put his head in her lap. If I could freeze time forever, that's where I'd stay.

On his last day, a Thursday in October, I lay on the dog bed next to him that morning and draped my arm around him until we fell asleep.

Dr. Fluke arrived in the afternoon. The three of us laughed and cried and told stories about this good old dog that we loved.

Alix and I held him in our laps. He looked tired, but he wagged his tail and relaxed in our arms. Dr. Fluke gave him one shot to make him sleep, and another to make him still.

It is almost eight years later as I write this, and sometimes even now, when we move a piece of furniture, we find a tuft of hair the color of beach sand.

7

THEY'RE ALL THERAPY DOGS

Everyone has something missing or something broken or something not quite fulfilled in their own life—but if they were to find the right dog, a dog that's alone and similarly incomplete, then together, as a unit, they would be made whole.

—Hrishikesh Hirway

And now we are back to Laura King and Striker, there in the tent at Westminster.

The show started with two thousand dogs. Striker beat all the other Samoyeds and all the winners from the Working Group. Now there are just seven dogs who can win Best in Show, and he is one of them again.

Laura doesn't own Striker. She handles dozens of dogs besides him. But one of the reasons they are here is that in the ring, each of them understands what the other one wants. For a few years, Jimmy Kimmel's late-night show had an annual bit where they showed clips from Westminster with the dogs digitally erased. The handlers moving around the ring alone look bizarre and awkward, contorting or listing to one side or shuffling to a peculiar beat. The truth, of course, is that the trip around the ring is about the dog, not the handler. All those strange moves serve the dog's gait. Despite how some handlers dress, the ultimate goal is the Kimmel bit in reverse: the handler erased from the picture, the dog making a perfect lap around the ring. A few times, I've watched Striker circle the ring without watching Laura. He's looked smooth and natural. But even when I've backed up and watched them both, she's never looked awkward. They have learned how to move together, side by side, like ice dancers.

Sometimes when I watched them I thought about Henry Aaron, my all-time favorite baseball player, the man who dethroned Babe Ruth as the home run king. Some people used to criticize Aaron because he never looked like he was hustling. What they did not understand was that he had worked so hard to learn the game that he always had a jump on a fly ball, always had the correct lead off first base, never overswung the bat even though he hit 755 home runs. He made his effort look effortless. That's what Laura and Striker did.

The effortless feel comes from countless practice and conditioning. Some handlers have their dogs run on treadmills, but Laura thinks that works better for little dogs. She just lets Striker run around outside as much as he wants when they're back home in Illinois. The rest is show practice. Her college degree was in exercise physiology. She believes in the power of muscle memory. So they practice their moves, over and over, until Striker's body has memorized what she wants him to do.

"So little of what happens in the ring is about what happens in the ring," she says. "I don't know if that makes any sense. But you get two or three minutes each time you're in the ring to be really strongly evaluated. We have to spend about twenty-three hours and whatever of the day making sure that those two or three minutes are perfect."

Right now Laura and Striker don't have twenty-three hours. It's closer to twenty-three minutes. The final seven dogs and their handlers linger backstage in the ready room inside the big tent on the lawn of the great estate. It's ten thirty at night, and Laura and her crew have been here since five thirty this morning. Laura is ragged and exhausted and exhilarated and calm, all at the same time. The calm comes from her dance partner. She has done this with Striker hundreds of times, maybe thousands. Right now he is standing loose and still, a fixed point in the universe as the handlers and caterers and TV producers whirlwind around him. If anything troubles him, it does not show. It could be any one of those nights at any one of those shows all over the country. Laura knows this one is different. She knows this is the last time she and Striker will ever be together like this.

Laura has tried not to let any of her worries travel down the leash. Even with all Striker's success, it has been a tough few years. COVID struck just as she and Striker were getting started. Her mother—who took her to those first few dog shows—died that same year. Laura's grandmother, too. So Laura has tried to remember to appreciate these times of joy and anticipation. In one of our conversations, she said her goal was to "just be here now, enjoy this for what it is, enjoy the dog for what it is and go with that."

The TV people are starting to line up the dogs for their moment in the spotlight. In the tent they are showing a montage of previous Best in Show winners. A crackle of tension is in the air. I think about Laura trying to live in the moment. It's not clear how much dogs actually live in the moment, but they seem to be a lot better at it than we are. Striker looks like he's waiting for a bus. Laura looks down at him and takes a deep breath.

Five minutes to go.

For thousands of years, we bred dogs for blue-collar jobs. Dogs herded sheep and cattle, exterminated rats and badgers, guarded forts and castles, pulled sleds and wagons, fought bulls and bears, fetched doves and ducks. They spent their lives outdoors. We treasured them for their strength and courage.

All those skills are still down in their DNA somewhere, but they go unused, like old water skis in a garage. Most dogs spend so much of their lives indoors or behind fences. We treasure them for what we perceive as their love and loyalty, and how they keep us unalone.

"Unalone." Such a lovely word. I first heard it in an unlikely place: the first *John Wick* movie. Keanu Reeves has made four of them so far, and they have grossed more than $1 billion at the box office. If you haven't seen the movies, you might not know that the inciting event of the whole series is a dog story. Here's a dog-centric *John Wick* synopsis:

A middle-aged retiree was grieving. His wife had just died after a long illness. She had arranged to give him one final gift and had written a note to go with it:

John, I'm sorry I can't be there for you. But you still need something, someone, to love. So start with this.

John wept as he put down the note and looked at the pet crate that came with it. Inside was a beagle puppy named Daisy.

John and Daisy bonded.

One day John was filling up his Mustang at a gas station when another car pulled up to the pumps. By chance it turned out that the men in the car were Russian mob thugs. One of them, the mob boss's son, came over to admire John's car. He asked John to name a price for it. John said it was not for sale. This upset the mob boss's son.

That night the thugs broke into John's house, beat him senseless, and took his car. During the beating, Daisy ran through the room whimpering. The mob boss's son told one of the thugs to shut her up.

When John regained consciousness, he saw a trail of blood on the floor. Daisy had crawled to him and died by his side.

That was the moment John Wick decided to come out of retirement and return to his life as the world's most feared assassin.

He went after the mob boss but was captured. The mob boss, as he prepared to have John killed, expressed disbelief: All this for a dog?

John replied: "When Helen died, I lost everything, until that dog arrived on my doorstep. A final gift from my wife. In that moment, I received some semblance of hope. An opportunity to grieve unalone."

Moments later he escaped his captors and resumed his trail of vengeance.

According to online tallies, during the course of four movies, John Wick has gone on to kill 439 people—including, and especially, the Russian mob thugs.

You do not fuck with a man's therapy dog.

• • •

"Some people get dogs for simpler reasons—for company, security, hunting, or work—with few psychological motives," says author Jon Katz in his 2004 book *The New Work of Dogs*. "But more people than ever see dogs as partners or surrogates as they deal with serious problems in their past or current lives."

Dogs now serve as grief counselors, conversation partners, roommates, and BFFs. A dog will never spill your darkest secret. A dog will lick your face in joy on your shittiest day. Some dogs dig holes for fun. But now their greatest skill is *filling* holes—the holes deep inside us.

Since 2011, American Humane—an animal welfare nonprofit—has named a Hero Dog of the year. The 2023 winner was a 150-pound Great Dane from Missouri named Maverick. Maverick works mostly with service members and their families. He visits schoolkids who are struggling with their classes. He welcomes troops home at USO locations. He stops by military bases when someone on the base dies unexpectedly. He goes to funerals with their families.

If you have spent time around a Great Dane, you will not be surprised at that gentleness. They are sweet and goofy and adorable, unless one of them is squishing the life out of you as it moves in for a cuddle. But Great Danes were never made for such things. They were bred in the sixteenth century to be hunting dogs—specifically, to catch a big animal like a boar and hold it down until the hunter could kill it. That requires a breathtaking combination of speed and power.

(I have to stop here for just a second to tell you that Great Danes have no particular connection to Denmark—they were developed in Germany. One story goes that they got the name because a French naturalist saw one in Denmark and called it Grand Danois, or Big Danish.)

Great Danes were made to capture wild beasts, not to calm troubled schoolchildren. In fact, almost no dog breed was developed for expertise in psychology. But human needs changed over the centuries. And if dogs are skilled at any one thing, it is understanding human needs.

To make an obvious point: many people don't feel any kinship with dogs at all. They fear dogs, or hate them, sometimes with good reason.

On the mildest end of the spectrum, some people have no tolerance for how dogs invade their personal space. A dog needing attention can suck the oxygen out of a room in a hurry. And a dog that hasn't been trained to chill can be overwhelming. Most dogs are not great at first impressions.

I tend to think of encounters with a dog the same way I think about drinking bourbon. That first swallow can be a little harsh. The second sip, once you're used to it, is a taste of the divine.

But a truly bad encounter with a dog can cause trauma that's hard to shake. Dogs can be aggressive, even if the aggression is friendly, and many of them have no sense of interpersonal space. If you're fearful, it can be hard to tell if they want to lick your face or go for your throat. Stephen King, who knows what scares people better than anyone else alive, pitted a rabid Saint Bernard against a mother and son trapped in a broken-down car in his 1981 novel *Cujo*. King was well aware that there are few things as terrifying as a big dog out of control.

(I don't think anything about a forty-year-old work qualifies as a spoiler alert, but heads up: they softened the ending of *Cujo* for the movie version. In the film, the little boy lives. In the book, he dies. Stephen King can be one ruthless bastard.)

Dogs have been used as weapons in conflicts throughout history. Some accounts say that Christopher Columbus was the first to use dogs in war in the New World, especially in battles with natives on the island of Hispaniola in the Caribbean. Ponce de León owned a famous mastiff mix named Becerrillo ("little bull"), which terrorized Puerto Rico and Bimini as de León conquered those territories. One story goes that in a single battle in Bimini, Becerrillo killed thirty-three natives.

In more modern times, civil rights protestors in the '60s had to contend with police dogs set upon them by bigots like Bull Connor, the police commissioner in Birmingham, Alabama. One of the signature photos in civil rights history, taken by Bill Hudson of the Associated Press during a protest in 1963, showed a Birmingham police dog lunging at the belly of a Black teenager named Walter Gadsden. "The image of the savage attack struck like lightning in the American mind," wrote historian Taylor Branch, and you can draw a line from that photo to the Civil Rights Act of 1964.

In 2020, after George Floyd was killed by police in Minneapolis, protestors marched all over the country, including outside the White House. Then-president Donald Trump tweeted that protestors were lucky they didn't breach the fence: "they would have been greeted with the most vicious dogs, and most ominous weapons, I have ever seen." Trump surely knew the echoes of America's past. And he also knew that to many people, "vicious dogs" and "ominous weapons" are synonyms.

Dogs are often a reflection of us. And we are sometimes broken mirrors.

So let's stipulate, as they say in court, that dogs are not therapeutic for everyone. But they are definitely therapeutic for millions and millions of people around the world. All types of dogs, big and small, elegant and slobbery, purebreds and mutts, have become humanity's unofficial therapists. Somewhere back in the deep distance, an early man (or early woman) noticed that things just felt better with a dog around. And at some point they issued what might have been the first dog command:

Stay.

We are still learning why and how dogs seem to understand us so well. Some studies have shown that dogs are deeply tuned in to our facial expressions and body language. They can tell our feelings and intentions from the arch of an eyebrow or the angle of our stance. We also know they can read us at a deeper, more chemical level. Dogs' noses pick up scents far beyond the range of what humans can smell. In the late '80s, two British dermatologists noticed that a patient's dogs kept sniffing a mole on her thigh. One of the dogs acted like it wanted to bite the mole off. It turned out the mole was melanoma. Further studies have shown that dogs can smell the organic compounds given off by not just several types of cancer, but also everything from diabetes to Parkinson's disease. This is scientific confirmation of what dog owners know from experience: a dog can tell when you're sick.

In Dogland, it's obvious how well dogs are tuned to their humans. A handler can train a show dog to respond to a little click of the tongue or a subtle tug on the lead. The dogs know when to run and when to stop running. They know when to freeze into a stack.

But show dogs have to practice those skills every day. Not only that, but their breeding probably fine-tunes those skills, like a high-end stereo system. The longer I spent around those dogs, the more I thought about dogs outside the show ring—what we think of as "normal" dogs. Those dogs have to figure out what their owners need, even if they don't get regular training, and even if it has nothing to do with why their breed was created. They have to improvise, as do their humans. So I talked to a couple of dog owners you might have heard of.

Tressie McMillan Cottom is one of America's sharpest minds. She's a sociologist, a professor at the University of North Carolina at Chapel Hill, a columnist for the *New York Times*, and a recipient of a MacArthur "genius grant." She has spoken and written beautifully and thoughtfully on everything from the unfair standards of beauty for women (especially Black women) to the populist magic of Dolly Parton. If you drafted guests for a dinner party, she'd be a first-round pick.

And yet she has also become discombobulated, captivated, and bumfuzzled by a Havanese* named Kirby.

"This dog is chaos in a furball form," she says. "I don't even remember why Kirby happened. I've blacked out the whole

---

*Havanese: Lapdog native to Cuba. Began to flourish in the US when refugees fled here after Fidel Castro took over in 1959. Known for comic timing and ability to learn tricks. AKC history page calls them "small, clever dogs that did no useful work."

experience of deciding to get Kirby. I blame COVID, I blame isolation, I blame so many things."

As she keeps talking about it, she decides that "blame" is not quite the right word. The conventional wisdom is that people get dogs to bring joy into their lives. Cottom's theory is that most people who get dogs are already happy. The dog is a symbol of their happiness.

Whatever the reason, late in 2021, she decided she needed a dog. She had bad allergies and a small yard, so that narrowed down the choices. She found a Havanese breeder in Charlotte, her hometown. They had a puppy the breeder had named Kobe, after Kobe Bryant. As far as NBA legends go, Cottom leans more toward Allen Iverson. Kobe, as a name, would not do. But she wanted something close so the dog wouldn't get confused. She remembered a scene from the Eddie Murphy rom-com *Boomerang*: Murphy's character pretends to have lost a dog to get a beautiful woman's phone number. The imaginary dog is named Kirby.

Cottom says she is speaking with academic rigor when she gives her objective opinion that her dog is adorable. "People crawl over tables to get to Kirby," she says. Cottom's mother, Vivian, always swore she was afraid of dogs. Now Vivian takes Kirby on playdates, feeds him chicken from Bojangles, and lets him sleep in her bed. A group of neighbor kids offered to take him on walks. They brought him back happy and exhausted. After a while, they started asking for ten bucks for the walks. They took PayPal. "I know a protection racket when I see one," Cottom says.

Cottom makes her living paying attention to how people behave and what that behavior means. She has noticed that Kirby changes her life from the outside in and from the inside out. White people feel more comfortable with her when she has Kirby around. She can wander into public spaces with less suspicion. This is objectively terrible but academically interesting. Kirby has a smoothing effect. Simply having a dog makes her more palatable to a world that can be hostile to outspoken women of color.

She has noticed that he smooths her, too. She jokes that she's so lazy that when dating sites ask for her preferred level of activity, she types "none." But Kirby has to go outside. He has a social calendar. He forces her out of the house. Before, when she pulled a long shift of writing or research, she would forget to eat or drink. But now she has to stop to feed Kirby, or get him some water, and it's often then that she notices she's hungry and thirsty, too: "Taking care of him, perversely, has helped me take a little better care of myself."

The gift of paying attention can be a curse. When you see things closely, analyzing them on the fly, it can be hard to just enjoy the moment. Dogs have some sense of the past, and—who knows?—maybe they dream of the future. But their lives are mostly about now. A dog drags you into the present tense.

Still, Cottom drifts among the tenses. She thinks about what her life was like before Kirby. She wonders what her life will be like without him. She jokes about eating worse and feeding him better so they die at the same time. Cottom was an only child. She was married once but has spent much of her life living alone. She says she did not acquire Kirby to fill any particular hole in her life. A symbol of her happiness, remember?

But.

"I did feel, however, like my life was—"

She pauses.

"I had more going out than I had coming in. There was just so much going out, out, out. Even when I liked it, or it was what I wanted, there was nothing coming in. I will say Kirby might be the only thing in my life that brings things in instead of just taking things out."

When they first started living together, he would race into the bedroom when she first stirred in the morning. She did not want company right then. Slowly, he learned. Now he knows to wait until the automatic coffee grinder starts. That means she's getting up for real. That's when he flies in. That's when she welcomes him. And they start another day together.

"I apologize in advance for however this goes," Scott Van Pelt said to the camera, because he knew he was about to cry.

It was the night of April 30, 2022. Van Pelt was anchoring the midnight edition of *SportsCenter*, the signature show on ESPN. He's the sports version of Conan or Letterman, the guy who wraps up the day with highlights and interviews and a couple of laugh lines. He loves his Maryland Terrapins and sympathizes with gamblers who take a bad beat. He gives off the aura of a guy you want to hang out with. Maybe watch a game and eat some wings. He is also supremely professional, one of the best in the world at his job, used to dealing with highly emotional moments. But not one like this.

Van Pelt has a regular feature on *SportsCenter* called One Big Thing, where he does an extended riff on a sports story he finds important or interesting. On this night, One Big Thing was not about sports. It was about a Rhodesian ridgeback named Otis.

Van Pelt's regulars know about Otis. During the pandemic,

when Van Pelt did interviews from his home office, Otis would be in the background over his right shoulder, curled up in his favorite leather chair, breaking it in like a catcher's mitt.

Van Pelt and his wife, Stephanie, got Otis two weeks after they got married: "training wheels before you have a kid . . . make sure you can take care of something, keep it alive." He was the last one left in the breeder's litter. Van Pelt thinks it's because he had a black nose and Rhodesians usually have a caramel nose. Dog people, as you know by now, can be picky that way.

Otis was there for the rise of Van Pelt's career, the birth of their three children, the move from Connecticut to the DC suburbs. He was the thread.

And now he was gone, and Van Pelt had written a script to talk about it. He faced the camera, not sure at all if he would make it through.

"The best part of this life is loving anything," he said. "And you do it even knowing the hardest part, which is that somewhere in the equation, inevitably, there will be loss."

Now, a month later, he's talking to me and there is another dog in the leather chair. This one isn't real. It's a giant stuffed dog Van Pelt won at an amusement park. It was one of those carny basketball games where the goal is twelve feet high and the rim is out of round. He gave it a try anyway, for the kids. Bottom of the net.

The dog has no name but his jersey says OTIS. It's the jersey of the US men's national soccer team. Gregg Berhalter, the head coach, sent it to him. Van Pelt doesn't know Berhalter, but the gift moved him deeply. And the stuffed dog sitting there in Otis's old spot feels reassuring. It's not an empty space.

Van Pelt is feeling overwhelmed. Millions of people watched

the tribute on Twitter. Thousands sent letters and emails. He was in Tulsa to cover the PGA Championship golf tournament, and a guy walked up to him in a bar, raised his drink, and said: "To Otis." Van Pelt jokes with his wife that they have the world's most famous dead dog.

Remembering helps. They remember that first night they brought him home, how he wouldn't walk on the hardwood floor in the kitchen, so Scott put him on a blanket and he walked to the end, and they kept moving it until Otis made it to the next room. They did not want him to sleep with them, but Otis had other plans. This became a bit of a problem when he grew to one hundred pounds. Sometimes he tried to push Stephanie out of the bed. She had her moments with him, their little routines together, but Scott was Otis's guy.

When Scott started on the late shift, he routinely got home at one thirty or two in the morning. The house would be dark except for a light in the kitchen. Scott would walk through to his office, still wound up from the show and needing to decompress. Otis would barrel down the stairs to meet him and headbutt Scott's leg until he got some treats. Then he'd hang out while Scott watched TV, or played an old NCAA football video game, or just caught his breath in the near dark.

The Van Pelt kids could wrestle with Otis or just pound on his sides like a bongo and it never fazed him. But one day, when Scott's heart rate spiked and they called for an ambulance, Otis jumped on the bed between him and the paramedics until he was convinced they weren't a threat. Another time, when an off-leash dog wandered near the house, Otis ran after it so hard he tore his ACL.

He ended up spending a lot of time at the vet. He kept growing lipomas—fatty lumps that aren't dangerous in and of themselves but can cause trouble if they press on organs or nerves. Otis had multiple surgeries to get rid of them. When he was seven, he had one that required taking out his spleen. The doctors were sure that one was cancer, but it wasn't, and Scott decided right then to indulge Otis for however long he had left.

It turned out to be three years.

And then, one week, Otis started to have trouble peeing. They gave him medicine for a urinary infection, but it didn't help. So they saw a specialist. They found a tumor on his prostate, and more on his stomach and lungs. The Van Pelts had lived with Otis being sick or hurt for so long that it had started to feel normal. So when the vet said he had just a few days left, Scott thought: *What the fuck are you talking about?* But then they had decisions to make, and there wasn't much time.

They were picking up Otis from the specialist on Friday. Stephanie's brother was getting married on Sunday. Scott stayed behind. He grilled a batch of cheeseburgers and fed them to Otis all day Saturday. Then he flew to the wedding.

They had agreed that Tuesday would be Otis's last full day. The Van Pelts live near Congressional Country Club, one of the top golf courses in America. One of Otis's favorite things was to ride around in a golf cart. So Congressional sent over a cart and Scott spent the day driving him up and down the street. Later on, when the kids got home from school, they did ride-alongs. As the light faded, Scott pulled the cart into the garage. Otis had always jumped out of the cart the moment they stopped. But this time he stayed there, curled up on Scott's lap. They lingered like that for nearly an hour. Then Scott had to go to work.

He got home and they had one more night together there in the office. At four thirty in the morning, Scott went up the stairs to bed. Otis climbed behind him, laboring. Scott turned around and held his dog and cried.

The next day, Scott and Stephanie were downstairs with Otis, waiting for the vet from a service called Lap of Love, when Otis clambered up the stairs again. Scott found him curled up on the ottoman at the foot of their bed. He knew what they say about how dogs will leave when it's time for them to die. Scott called Otis to come back down with him. Otis just lowered his head. Scott will never know for sure. But he believes Otis knew it was time.

"There have been a couple of moments after he died that you just come in and sit there and know that he's not coming and it's just—"

"That absence, right?" I say.

"Oh, God, it's so heavy," he says. "I've lost people. I've lost my dad and I've lost grandparents and it's not comparative, but the difference is that this animal was with us every day of our life and in all ways of our life and was here every moment of our children's lives. He's the corner puzzle piece. So many things connect to that. You could put your whole puzzle together and there's that one corner that's missing."

The kids rebounded faster than Scott and Stephanie did. A few days after Otis died, they started asking about a new dog. Scott needed more time. He held out four months. They got a puppy. Another Rhodesian ridgeback. They named him Redd, as in Redding, as in Otis Redding. A convoluted callback to the old dog they had loved.

Right after they got him, Scott was a guest on the Ringer's video interview show *Slow News Day*. As he talked to host Kevin Clark, there in the home office, Redd wandered into the background and took a dump on the floor. Scott called for a time-out.

A few months later, Redd somehow escaped from his doggy daycare and scared the hell out of the family before he was found. But otherwise things have gone great. Redd is goofy and loving and reminds them of Otis all the time. A few months after they got him, Scott texted me a photo of Redd glaring through a glass door at a deer outside with this caption: *Currently filled with seething rage*.

At one point, back when we were talking about Otis, Scott said dogs are dessert. There's all the other stuff you have to do in life, and then dogs are the cookies and ice cream. All Scott had to do was be happy, and that would make Otis happy, and then they would both be even happier. An unadulterated good. Dessert.

The truth is we both know better. Cookies don't get sick. You don't watch ice cream die. Maybe this is the thing that twists up our insides so much: dogs can *feel* like a trifle, right up to the moment when you realize their very presence has changed you. Maybe this is why the emotion can get so out of whack, why so many people cry harder over a dog than over the people they love. Any relationship with another human being is complicated. But losing a dog snatches away something pure. The loss of a family member *means* more. The loss of a dog can *hurt* more.

Scott and I had been talking a while. I had asked him two or three times what made Otis so important in his life and his family's life. He came at it a few different ways. But then he reduced it to a couple of sentences.

"We thought Otis to be this special thing because he was *our* special thing," he said. "All a dog has to do is just be yours."

Scientists weren't all that interested in dogs as a topic of study until the last fifty years or so. They're not exotic like gorillas. They're not endangered like bison. But starting in the '80s, researchers started figuring out that the interaction between humans and animals was worth looking into. That led to the creation of a field called anthrozoology.

Since then, studies have explored the connection between dogs and people from hundreds of different angles. If you have spent much time in academia, you know there is always research to back up whatever point of view you might have. It's no different when it comes to dogs.

Many studies have shown that having a dog is excellent for your health. There's one obvious reason—a dog keeps you active. You have to make sure it gets exercise, which means you probably get some exercise, too. A dog also requires a daily routine, and that adds structure to your life. So some research has concluded that dog owners are less likely to die of a heart attack or stroke. They also improve the mood of people with chronic pain.

But there are countering studies that conclude the health benefits of having a dog are, at best, inconclusive. Depressed people don't necessarily get happier from having a dog. Sick children don't get significantly better. Even official emotional support dogs don't appear to make that much difference to many people who need emotional support. Is a dog in your life real nourishment, or just cotton candy? To science, the jury's still out.

What interests me more is that researchers are now looking through the other end of the telescope—how the dog feels about all this.

There doesn't appear to be much research about show dogs specifically. But there's ample research now about dogs in general, and again, it covers a wide range of conclusions. One study showed that when dogs and people gaze at each other, they both get a dose of oxytocin—the "happiness hormone." Another study showed that when given a choice between human affection and a meal, dogs chose the affection just as often—in other words, they crave our love as much as they crave food. Which, for a dog, is saying something. But then again, in rebuttal: one study showed that dogs don't really feel guilty when they've done something we think of as bad. They just give us that "guilty" look when they can tell we're about to get mad at them.

Dog cognition expert Alexandra Horowitz runs the Dog Cognition Lab at Barnard College and has written four books about the lives of dogs and their bond with humans. She has popularized the concept of *umwelt* (pronounced *OOM-velt*), first coined by a German biologist to define how an animal experiences life. Part of it is basic input: dogs can hear tones we can't and smell a far wider range of odors and aromas. Their sensory world overlaps with ours but doesn't match. But beyond that, *umwelt* refers to a dog's inner life: what it needs and wants, how it goes about getting those things, and how it feels about the process.

I asked Horowitz the question that started my journey into Dogland: *Are show dogs happy?* I wondered if, to her, as a dog expert, the question made any sense.

"I think this is a perfectly reasonable question, and absolutely the right question to ask," she said. "Insofar as dogs are sentient beings who do a hell of a lot for humans, I think we owe it to them to be concerned with their happiness, as far as possible."

Horowitz has been a strong advocate for understanding a dog's essential dogness. We put them by our sides and brought them into our homes, so we have a responsibility to understand them, instead of just understanding them through the filter of us. Along those lines, she wonders if the dog-show lifestyle is good for dogs. Show dogs are often confined in crates. They are constantly groomed and primped, and lots of dogs don't like that. Even though they're around other dogs all the time, there's not much of a chance to socialize.

But Horowitz also said: "Insofar as some handlers are going to have a very strong bond with their dogs, and vice versa, time with that handler will be positive time."

For the final round they bring the dogs out one by one. There is a false start: the handler for River, the German shepherd who won the Herding Group, heads down the aisle too early. It's not clear if this is the handler's fault or some TV producer's fault, but a woman with a headset screams: "Come back! Come back! Come back!" People in the grandstands laugh. It eases the tension in the tent. Although it probably did not ease the tension for River and his handler.

A minute later they start over, and River trots back out. Laura and Striker are next. Sam Hanle, one of Laura's assistants, has already put the gear in the box onstage: portable fan, spray bottle, lucky blue towel. Laura's got the comb under the rubber band on her arm. The lead is in her left hand, and Striker is quiet on the other end, waiting for his cue.

"The winner of the Working Group . . ."

They run down the tunnel and past the flowers and out onto the green carpet. Striker angles his head toward the crowd, watching as they cheer. A shared experience. A moment of hope and joy. A way to feel unalone.

Pee Break

ADVERTISING DOGS, RANKED

#5

Dogecoin

There was a meme involving the grammatically broken thoughts of a Shiba Inu* that became really popular around 2010. Two software engineers created a cryptocurrency with the dog (or "doge," which I am not going to begin to explain) as its mascot. They originally did this as a joke, but the currency ended up reaching a market cap of $85 billion. Elon Musk is planning a Dogecoin-funded trip to put a satellite on the moon. He briefly turned the Twitter logo into the Dogecoin logo before renaming the whole thing X. I want a time machine just to hear all this explained to someone in 1970.

*Shiba Inu (pronounce the *i*'s as *e*'s): Small white-bellied hunting dog that originated in Japan. Nearly became extinct after World War II. First came to America with a military family in 1954. Now Japan's top companion dog.

#4

Taco Bell Chihuahua

A bitch called Gidget (not named in the ads) was the star of Taco Bell commercials from 1997 to 2000, fueled by the phrase "*¡Yo quiero Taco Bell!*" ("I want some Taco Bell!"). Hispanic groups complained about the cultural stereotype and the company phased out the campaign. The ads with the dog wearing a Che Guevara beret might have been slightly over the top.

#3

Lady Greyhound

The Greyhound bus line introduced a live mascot in 1957 after going decades without one. She was originally named Steverino after appearing on *The Steve Allen Show*, then was later renamed Lady Greyhound. She visited the White House, posed with Miss Universe contestants, and wore a diamond collar and tiara. The legend goes that she traveled by plane because Greyhound didn't allow dogs on its buses.

#2

Spuds MacKenzie

A sunglasses-wearing bull terrier who became a huge star of Bud Light commercials from 1987 to 1989. Spuds was "one party-loving happening dude" who had three gorgeous women as his chorus of sorts as he romped poolside or played slide guitar at a ski lodge. Opponents (including Senator Strom Thurmond of South Carolina) complained that Spuds made drinking look like fun to children. Somewhere along the way, an even deeper scandal was revealed: Spuds MacKenzie, the party dude, was in real life a bitch named Evie from Illinois.

#1

Nipper

A British painter named Francis Barraud inherited a terrier mix named Nipper that had belonged to his late brother. The dog died in 1895, but Barraud kept thinking about how Nipper would listen to music with his head cocked to the side. A few years later, Barraud made a portrait of Nipper listening to an early cylinder phonograph invented by Thomas Edison. He sold the image to the Gramophone Company in Liverpool after changing the cylinder phonograph into one of the company's new record players. RCA acquired the American rights in 1929, and the Nipper painting—called *His Master's Voice*—became one of the most recognizable company logos in world history. A stained-glass version from an old RCA headquarters building is on display at the Smithsonian.

8

THE HEART-DOG

I told him about the way they get to know you. Not the way people do, the way people flatter you by wanting to know every last thing about you, only it isn't a compliment, it is just efficient, a person getting more quickly to the end of you. Correction—dogs *do* want to know every last thing about you. They take in the smell of you, they know from the next room, asleep, when a mood settles over you. The difference is there's not an end to it.

—Amy Hempel, "The Dog of the Marriage"

The seven finalists for Best in Show at Westminster 2022:

Striker, the Samoyed, winner of the Working Group. Six-year-old dog. Handled by Laura King of Milan, Illinois. Registered name: GCHP CH Vanderbilt 'N Printemp's Lucky Strike. If you are just now learning all this, shame on you for skipping to this part of the book. Number of Samoyeds that have won Westminster: 0.

River, the German shepherd, winner of the Herding Group. Five-year-old dog. Handled by Lenny Brown of Jasper, Georgia.

Registered name: GCHG CH Gem-N-I River of Urloved CGC. Number of German shepherds that have won Westminster: 2.

Trumpet, the bloodhound, winner of the Hound Group. Four-year-old dog. Handled by Heather Buehner of Berlin Center, Ohio. Registered name: GCHB CH Flessner's Toot My Own Horn. Number of bloodhounds that have won Westminster: 0.

Belle, the English setter, winner of the Sporting Group. Four-year-old bitch. Handled by Amanda Ciaravino of Pine Island, Minnesota. Registered name: GCHS CH Ciara N' Honeygait Belle of the Ball FDC CGC. Number of English setters that have won Westminster: 1.

MM, the Lakeland terrier, winner of the Terrier Group. Six-year-old bitch. Handled by Ariel Cukier of Greenwood, Delaware. Registered name: GCHG CH Hi-Kel Terrydale Nanhall Mizzconceived. Number of Lakeland Terriers that have won Westminster: 2.

Winston, the French bulldog, winner of the Non-Sporting Group. Three-year-old dog. Handled by Perry Payson of Bixby, Oklahoma. Registered name: GCHP CH Fox Canyon's I Won the War at Goldshield CGCA CGCU TKN. Number of French Bulldogs that have won Westminster: 0.

Hollywood, the Maltese, winner of the Toy Group. Three-year-old bitch. Handled by Tim Lehman of Hastings-on-Hudson, New York. Registered name: GCHB CH Ta-Jon's Walk of Fame. Number of Maltese that have won Westminster: 0.

Vegas doesn't take bets on Westminster. But if they did, there would be three clear favorites.

Terriers have won Best in Show at Westminster forty-eight times—more than a third of all winners. MM (pronounced *Em*) has history on her side.

Winston became the first French bulldog to reach number one in the all-breed rankings, timing it perfectly with the Frenchie becoming the most popular dog in America. There is also this: the man who will judge Best in Show is a Frenchie owner. (We'll meet him in a second.) It's not an official conflict of interest—there's no direct connection to Winston—but the judge obviously likes Frenchies. Or at least *his* Frenchie.

The third favorite is Striker.

It's his second year in a row in the final group. He was the all-breeds number one in 2021 and has been near the top of the list this year. He is also the favorite of the *New York Times* livebloggers covering the event. They have six reporters following along, either here at Lyndhurst or on TV, and they have come to a clear consensus. One of the livebloggers, Benjamin Hoffman, writes: "Striker, or we riot."

Now, on the FOX Sports broadcast, a black SUV limo pulls into Lyndhurst. Westminster treats the Best in Show judge like a juror in a murder trial. The judge is stashed in a hotel during the show and is prohibited from finding out news about the winners. The idea is to have no preconceptions. Westminster announced who would judge Best in Show nearly a year ago. Everybody in the building knows the identity of the judge. But only now will Don Sturz find out which dogs he will choose from to crown a champion. He steps out of the limo, tuxedoed and smiling.

Sturz is sixty and his day job is superintendent of a school system on Long Island. He started showing dogs when he was ten, partly as an escape from school, where he says he was often bullied. He has been a dog-show judge for thirty-two years. He has judged breed and group rounds at Westminster, and he was an on-camera analyst for their TV coverage. He knows the show about as well as anyone alive. Jamie Little, the in-ring reporter, corrals him for an interview before the group winners come out.

"This is the moment of a lifetime for me," he says. "I'm thrilled and also humbled by the responsibility."

Now everything is ready. The crowd goes quiet. The announcer calls out the dogs.

They're ordered biggest to smallest, so the short-legged dogs don't hold up the long-legged ones. River the German shepherd comes out after his false start. Then Striker. Trumpet, the bloodhound. Belle, the English setter. MM, the Lakeland. Winston, the Frenchie. Hollywood, the Maltese.

The handlers lead the dogs to their bright-yellow boxes with the names of the breeds in purple letters. Laura swings Striker around to the SAMOYED box. It will take Sturz about half an hour to inspect all the dogs and make his choice. Much of Laura's life, and most of Striker's, has funneled down to this half hour. It is the last time Striker will ever do this. The last time he and Laura will go around the ring together.

As they wait to be called, Laura feels a tug on the lead. Striker is straining, looking off to his left and behind him. This moment, of all moments, he needs to be still and focus. But instead he's distracted. Something has his full attention.

From the moment they met, she did everything for him. That's not always how it worked. Laura had handled other dogs that performed better if she was a guest star. Her assistants took care of the dogs day to day, then Laura got to play grandma—swoop in, run the dogs around the show ring, then hand them off again. The dog show was their special time together. That method won a lot of ribbons and trophies, especially with younger dogs. But Striker had already run a campaign up in Canada. He had been to plenty of dog shows. He knew the routines. What he did not know was Laura. She decided the important thing with him was to form a deeper connection.

So she put him out in the morning. She cleaned his crate. She fed him and got him water. She groomed him and bathed him and trimmed his nails. She was the one who touched him and talked to him. She taught Striker that she belonged to him as much as he belonged to her. And along the way, she began to realize she had fallen in a certain kind of love.

Love is a tricky thing to talk about in Dogland. You'd think it would be easy, given how dog people profess love for their dogs. At every dog show you can buy sweatshirts or bumper stickers or refrigerator magnets with endless variations of "I ❤ my [your breed here]." Of course the people in the show world love dogs in the abstract. It would make no sense to put in the hours otherwise. But the nature of the work makes it tough to form a deep relationship with any particular dog. If you're showing twenty dogs in a weekend, your attention is bound to be divided. At the professional level, a show dog is a gig a handler takes on for money. The humans involved are clear-eyed about it. The dogs might wonder what the hell is going on, but if dogs have learned anything, it is how to adapt. The brutal math of a dog show means that loving has to sit with losing. There is no breed standard for love. Only one dog wins it all.

Part of Laura's job is shaping ordinary dogs into something

special, and shaping special dogs into champions. It's what she thinks of as the measure of a pro. But being a pro also means paying attention to what the dog wants. She once handled the number one Beauceron* in the country. He was physically beautiful in every way, and happy almost all the time, except when they got to the show ring. One morning the Beaucerons were being judged early and they were there for the national anthem. There was a little feedback from the speakers, and somebody dropped something nearby, and the dog freaked out. Laura thought about it, wondered if it was just a one-time thing. In the end she decided he just hated his job. "He doesn't give a shit about being in here, so why would we make him do it?" she said. "So we sent him home."

Every handler remembers those near misses, the dogs that had the desire but not the talent, or the talent but not the desire. Laura has won hundreds of Best in Shows. She and Robin have made a healthy living, enough to have Betty White and the spread in Illinois. But she has had lots of near misses, too. And she's never had the best of the best until Striker.

She still works with other dogs because she likes the owners, or she thinks the dogs have potential, or because she needs to pay the bills. She has the perspective and detachment necessary to see Dogland in all its shades. But when she talks about Striker, her body language changes. Inside that rational heart, you can hear tumblers turning.

---

*Beauceron: Sheepherding dog from France—over there they call it *bas-rouge* ("red stocking") for its rust-colored feet. Colette, the French novelist you might remember as loving her frog-faced Frenchie, said her Beauceron was "one of those rare companions who remain silent at the right time, respect our work and our sleep, howl for our own tears, and close their eyes with a bitter discretion in the face of anything—the kiss of a lover, the tender hug of a child—that deprives them of our fickle human friendship."

• • •

There is a concept among dog people called the heart-dog. The origin isn't clear, but the meaning is. The heart-dog is a soulmate, a once-in-a-lifetime experience, a memory that throbs in your mind long after others have flattened into a scrapbook. The heart-dog is the one that maybe makes you sound a little crazy when you talk about it.

Most dog lovers own just a few dogs in the course of their lives. It's easier to have a heart-dog because they get to spend so much time with each one. For dog handlers it's different. They have hundreds of dogs breeze through their lives, maybe thousands. Some they meet for only a weekend. Others might stick around a few months. But even some long-term connections are just working relationships. The heart-dog is a lightning strike, the swelling strings of an orchestra, an Outer Banks beach as the sun comes up. Even trying to write about it coats the page with sap. It can be embarrassing to wake up one day and realize you have given so much of yourself to another living creature. It can also be thrilling to give so much of yourself to anything at all. The thing about a dog is, it almost always gives back. People have heart-cats and heart-parrots and there are probably a few heart-turtles out there. But people and dogs have built their relationship over tens of thousands of years. We have used one another for our mutual benefit. But at some point, it can't be just that. The heart has to get involved.

Laura spent all that time with Striker early on because she decided that's what it would take to make him a champion. The results suggest she was right. But she also spent a lot of time around him because it made her feel good.

"I get encouragement from him, too, because he is such a happy dog," she says. "On the days where you're like, 'Oh God, I have to do this again,' he's just like, 'Yes, let's go, let's go, let's go.'"

This is part of what we look for in love, no? Somebody to help us through the hard times?

Most of the reality of Dogland has nothing to do with the swelling orchestra and the sunrise on the beach. It's more like a cold Thursday morning on the concrete floor of a civic center in a place you'd never heard of two months before. It takes something extra to get you through those moments. Coffee, sure. Grit, probably. A sense of responsibility. And, maybe, love.

I asked Laura at one point if Striker was her heart-dog. She took a long pause.

"Yes and no," she said.

Another pause.

"There's a part of you that's always more grounded in a job like mine. You know that you can't keep the dog forever. It's always in the back of your mind, or at least it's in the back of mine. But having said that . . . he is the most amazing dog. The cutest. The sweetest temperament. He's funny. We just connect on the deepest level. So I'm not sure if that's an answer."

Yeah. It's an answer.

The dogs are in a long line on one side of the ring. Sturz walks the line, from River down to Hollywood, then walks backward the other way. "OK, everybody up, we're gonna have some fun, we're gonna go around together," he says. The dogs do a lap around the ring as he watches. Laura has Striker focused, mostly, but every so often he twists around to look at whatever he's so interested in.

Now Sturz inspects the dogs one by one. As he looks at River, Laura spritzes Striker with water and combs his fur and tries to get him to settle. Sturz sends River down to the end of the ring and back. As he trots away, Laura and Striker step into the empty space. They're up next. This is the two minutes that count the most. The dog and the judge, one on one.

"An exceedingly close association with their people imprinted a wonderful temperament on the Samoyed," says Michael LaFave, the ring announcer.

Sturz checks Striker's neck, his teeth, his ears. "Samoyeds are willing to do any jobs asked of them," LaFave says at nearly the exact moment Sturz checks Striker's testicles. He stays still through all of it. No glancing around.

But then Laura walks him a few steps to the side for the down and back, and he's not paying attention. Laura grips his muzzle, bends down to talk to him. As they head to the other end of the ring, Striker spends the first few steps looking off to the side.

They get back and Sturz sends them on a lap around the ring, and that goes well. Striker glides. *Maybe we salvaged it*, Laura thinks.

The other five dogs take their turns. Sturz walks down the line, occasionally tilting his head like a—well, you know.

"Anything in any of the movement that caught your attention?" Chris Myers asks the veteran dog-show judge Jason Hoke on the TV broadcast.

"None of them gave him an out," Hoke says.

Sturz gives the dogs one last task. He asks the handlers to

bring them out one by one and do a natural stack—striking the pose without the handler's help. Then one more lap around the ring.

When it's Striker's turn, the crowd starts to laugh. He's dancing around. "Having a party," Hoke says. The master of the thousand-yard stare all of a sudden can't stand still. Sturz actually does a little *chk-chk-chk* with his tongue to get Striker to hold the stack for a second.

My friend Joe Posnanski, when he covered the 2000 Summer Olympics, ended up going on a whim to the Greco-Roman wrestling final. The gold-medal match featured Aleksandr Karelin, a Russian legend, who had never been beaten in thirteen years of international competition. His opponent was a Wyoming farm boy named Rulon Gardner. Joe didn't know the rules of Greco-Roman wrestling, and it was hard for him to tell what was going on beyond a lot of grunting and struggling. But all of a sudden there was a gasp from the crowd. Gardner had outmaneuvered Karelin somehow and he was up 1–0. I remember Joe telling me how he wasn't even sure what had happened, just that something shifted, and all of a sudden the match had changed for good.

That's sort of what it's like to watch Striker in this moment. The announcers don't appear to notice anything wrong, and if they do, they paper it over. But that laugh from the crowd feels like the gasp at the Olympic final. Something has shifted.

Sturz gives the dogs one last look, from a distance. Then he goes over to a table at the other side of the ring and fills out his ballot. There will be two names on it, one for Reserve Best in Show—the runner-up—and one for Best in Show.

Laura, like everyone else, has known for nearly a year that

Sturz would be the Best in Show judge. She has a lot of respect for him. She thinks he is a fair judge and a good man. She also thinks, if he leans any direction in particular, it's toward hounds.

Sturz picks up the giant golden Reserve Best in Show ribbon and walks to center stage with three other Westminster officials. Matt Flegenheimer of the *New York Times* says in the paper's live blog: "These four bow-tied gentlemen have nontrivial barbershop quartet energy."

The dogs and handlers stand in their line. After all the dancing, Striker now holds a perfect stack.

"Tonight," Sturz says, "Reserve Best in Show winner will be the French bulldog."

Winston bounds to the center of the ring, and Perry Payson accepts the ribbon. The number one dog in the country all year has finished second. Now the title is really up for grabs.

Sturz goes back to the table and picks up two more purple-and-gold ribbons. The other members of the barbershop quartet tote various trophies and silver cups and such.

"Six dogs standing," Jason Hoke says.

Sturz thanks the owners and breeders and handlers: "But most of all, I want to thank our dogs for the comfort and joy and love they bring to our everyday lives."

Striker, now still as a portrait. Laura, running her hand through his fur.

"The best in show winner is—"

Laura looks up.

"—the bloodhound."

Laura looks down and hugs Striker. Then she goes over to hug Heather, Trumpet's handler. The ring is filling up with people and

Striker is dancing again, ready to play. But Trumpet moves to the spot at center stage, over the rug with the likeness of Sensation, Westminster's perfect dog. The other dogs and their handlers drift to the edge. It is no longer their time. In what feels like seconds, the whole thing is over.

The PA is playing Sinatra's "New York, New York." Laura takes Striker back to the box with SAMOYED on the side. She picks up the water and the fan and the lucky blue towel, and they head back down the hallway while the party goes on.

Backstage there is a lot of hugging but not many tears. More than anything, Laura and Robin and their assistants are exhausted.

Striker is curled up in a battered crate with a LIVE ANIMAL sticker on the side. Another crate carries his prizes from winning the group—two more trophies and one last giant ribbon.

All of a sudden the sound of a hundred drum rolls echoes through the tent. A front has come through and it's pouring out-side. The tent is a good hundred yards from the van. You can see the whole crew go limp as they search for umbrellas and raincoats.

Laura thinks she knows what happened to Striker out there in the ring. It was the English setter, Belle. Belle looked like some of the English springer spaniels that Laura and Robin keep back in Illinois. They always have a bunch around, and there's almost always one in heat. Laura thinks Striker got fixated on Belle be-cause he thought it was one of the dogs from back home: "He was convinced that she was his girlfriend."

Not only did Striker have the wrong dog, he had the wrong breed of dog. Lust can make us do strange things.

This was, of course, a terrible break at the worst possible time. Maybe Striker would have won. No way of knowing. Sturz later told *Showsight* why he chose Trumpet: "He looked at me with a soulful expression and conveyed great pride and strength. Then he went around: powerful, ground-covering, and elastic."

Note that there was nothing in that description about the breed standard.

Whatever the reason, the bottom line is that, in the biggest moment of his career, Striker got weird. Not weird for a regular dog, but weird for a show dog.

In that moment he let go of years of training, generations of breeding, all that work humans did to create the Samoyed's wonderful stillness. Show dogs are bred and trained to produce predictability. But in that moment he became unpredictable. He derailed the plans his human had for him.

In short, for a few seconds, he turned into a real dog.

People in Dogland are quick to remind everyone that show dogs are pets when they're not in the ring. This is true. But when they *are* in the ring, they're expected to be something different, to rise above their doggish instincts, to prove why they were deemed show quality instead of pet quality.

There's no way to know if Striker felt that pressure, except to say that dogs have made it this far by sensing what humans are feeling. Maybe the stress of the moment led Striker to feel some kind of stress, too.

So much of what a handler teaches a dog is the willpower to accept delayed gratification. Hold this stack, stand still for the judge, trot around the ring like we practiced, and you get a treat. Waiting for a treat has to be hard as hell for a dog. It's hard enough for humans. We wreck our long-term goals all the time for short-term pleasures. We can't be surprised that a dog might do it, too, no matter how well trained.

It is funny to think that the final round of the most prestigious dog show in the world, a moment that the dogs and handlers had trained years for, might have swung on the fact that, at a crucial juncture, one of the dogs just really wanted to get laid.

Well, funny *now*, maybe. Not so funny then.

The drum rolls subside a little. The rain is slackening. One of the security guards wanders by and sees Striker in his crate. She bends down to get a closer look.

"He's so cute!" she says.

Laura tries to smile but can't quite get there. She grabs hold of the cart with Striker and the trophies and the gear. "We're gonna make a break for it," she says.

Everybody nods. They still have to pack the tables and the awnings and the grooming gear. They are driving back to Illinois in the morning.

They head down the ramp and into the rain and across the ruined grass. Safe in his crate, Striker has fallen asleep.

TRAVELING DOGS, RANKED

#5

Owney

Somewhere around 1888, a terrier mutt named Owney started walking to work with his owner, a clerk at the post office in Albany, New York. Owney loved sleeping on the mailbags and soon became the mascot of the post office. When the clerk quit, Owney stayed. Not long after, he started riding mail trains from town to town. The local post office would take care of him and attach a medal or tag to his collar to take back home. He rode the train for more than 140,000 miles and became famous along the way, traveling as far as Japan. He was shot and killed in Toledo, Ohio, in 1897—the details have never been clear, but the story went that he had attacked a clerk and US marshal at the post office there. After he died, postal clerks around the country begged that he be preserved instead of buried. His taxidermied remains are housed at the Smithsonian.

#4

Charley

John Steinbeck took his ten-year-old standard poodle with him in 1960 on his drive around America in a camper truck. The resulting book, *Travels with Charley*, became a number one bestseller in 1962. More recent analysis of the book casts doubts on whether everything in the book actually happened, but the trip itself definitely happened, and Charley was with Steinbeck as they visited thirty-seven states. In the book, he's an icebreaker for the people Steinbeck meets along the way and a listener as Steinbeck ruminates about his country. "In some areas," Steinbeck writes, "Charley is more intelligent than I am."

#3

Seaman

Not long before Lewis and Clark started their expedition across the West in 1804, Meriwether Lewis bought a Newfoundland named Seaman in Pittsburgh. Newfoundlands are known for their power and swimming ability, and Lewis figured both might be necessary for the trip. Seaman caught and killed much of the food that the Corps of Discovery ate along the way—squirrels, geese, deer, and even a pronghorn antelope. In 1806, as the expedition was headed back home, a group of Native Americans stole the dog, and Lewis sent three men after the thieves. They released Seaman once they were caught. After Lewis died in 1809—possibly by suicide—the story goes that Seaman refused to eat and died of grief. There are monuments to Seaman all over the country, including a sculpture that was displayed in the White House.

#2

Bobbie the Wonder Dog

In August 1923, the Brazier family of Silverton, Oregon, took a car trip to visit relatives in Wolcott, Indiana. They brought along their collie / English shepherd mix, Bobbie. But while they were in Indiana, three other dogs attacked Bobbie and he ran off. The family searched but could not find him and returned to Oregon heartbroken. Six months later, Bobbie turned up at their door. By all accounts he made the 2,500-mile trip by himself, crossing the Continental Divide in the middle of winter. According to later reports, he often showed up at service stations where the Braziers had stopped along the way. The story was featured in newspapers across the country, as well as in *Ripley's Believe It or Not!*, and Bobbie played himself in a silent film called *The Call of the West*.

#1

Laika

The first creature to orbit the Earth was an eleven-pound bitch found on the streets of Moscow. The Soviet program decided to put a dog into their *Sputnik 2* spacecraft in 1957, and Laika was one of three strays chosen as candidates—scientists figured strays would be used to harsh conditions. The idea was to monitor how she reacted to the launch and orbit, in hopes of future human spaceflight. But even though they provided enough food for seven days, the Russians did not expect Laika to survive that long—it was impossible at the time to keep the cabin from overheating. She died five or six hours into the flight, a thousand miles above the Earth.

9

SOMEWHERE IN MICHIGAN

Dogs come into our lives to teach us about love and loyalty.
They depart to teach us about loss.

—Erica Jong

It's a Sunday morning in September, not cold yet but you can feel it coming. The clouds spatter rain and you can smell coffee and dog shampoo. Three months ago the best show dogs in the country met at Westminster, under the big tent at Lyndhurst. Now a few of the best dogs, plus a lot of others, have gathered at the Shiawassee County Fairgrounds, north of the interstate between Lansing and Flint, for a series of shows called the Mid-Mitten Cluster. There's a tent here, too, but it's smaller and plainer, and the dog show rings are roughly on the same spot where a few weeks ago fairgoers held a cornhole tournament. There's no network TV coverage here, no judge in a tux, no majestic lawn rolling down to the Hudson. Just cornfields and soybeans and the Detroit Lions pregame on the radio.

Striker is the best show dog on the grounds. But most people don't even know he's here. He's not listed in the program. He won't appear in the ring. Laura and Robin have brought him here for a different reason.

Betty White is parked along a fence nearby. Most of Laura and Robin's show dogs are in crates in the back. A few are romping around in a row of ex-pens outside. Robin comes down the back stairs with Striker and lets him into one of the pens with a couple of smaller dogs. They take turns peeing in the same corner. Striker has what I can only describe as bedhead. His magnificent coat is matted on one side. You know how it is with retirees. Some of them just let themselves go.

A couple of other dogs walk past, on the other side of the RV, and Striker barks—nothing aggressive, just a hey-howya-doing thing, a quick sharp note that rises a little at the end. It startles me. I've been around Striker dozens of times. It's the first time I've ever heard him bark.

Does he know what's about to happen? Does he sense that *something* is about to happen?

Emily Dickinson once said of dogs, "They are better than (human) Beings—because they know—and do not tell."

I wonder if she got it backward. They tell, but we don't know.

Most professional dog handlers don't own their show dogs. The dogs stay with them, sometimes for years, while they travel the circuit together. But when the dog retires, it goes back to the people it officially belongs to. There is always a handoff. This is part of the business. Everybody understands how it works. Sometimes the handoff is a celebration of a good working relationship. Sometimes it's more of a relief. Sometimes it is complicated and bittersweet.

It can also be a rehearsal of sorts for the other big goodbye. The most cruel thing about loving an animal is that it is likely to die first. From the moment we take home a pet, we set a timer for heartbreak, because their life spans are shorter than ours. We often witness nearly their entire time on Earth, from wobbly birth to endless sleep. It is one reason some people don't have pets. They can't face knowing they will witness the end.

It might also be a reason those of us who love dogs love them so fiercely. Because we know they're going to leave us.

There are other shows all around the country this weekend—Alabama, Colorado, New Jersey, Oklahoma, Oregon—but Laura and Robin came here because this is the show closest to Toronto. Marc Ralsky and Correen Pacht, two of Striker's owners, have driven down from there for the weekend. They are here to pick up Striker and complete his transition from a show dog into a pet.

Striker stayed one night in their hotel room, just to get acclimated, but he has spent most of the weekend with Laura and Robin. They tried to make his last full day with them normal but also special. He didn't sleep in his crate—they gave him the run of Betty White. That morning he went over to Laura's side of the bed and huffed until she got up, laughing. She didn't make any big plans. They just hung out together, like they had when they first met, when all she wanted was for them to make a connection. That was two years and eight months ago. They won 111 shows together, trained for countless hours, rode tens of thousands of miles, followed the fancy all over America.

On Saturday night Laura said her goodbyes. There was no big speech, no fancy words. Just a nice quiet night, holding him close.

She told herself that today would be business. She wants the handoff to be quick and easy. Better for everybody that way.

Laura and Robin have also brought their blue sprinter van, which somehow has gone unnamed. They needed two vehicles because Robin is going back home and Laura is headed to another show. But the van was also useful to haul their extra cargo: the awards and ribbons and trophies Laura and Striker had won together. Laura kept a few things back in Illinois. But most of the spoils belong to Striker's owners.

Judi Elford has come to Michigan, too. She and her husband also have an ownership stake in Striker. Plus, Judi was the breeder who picked Striker out of the litter six years ago. She's the one who decided he had show quality. Now Judi comes by the van to select some memorabilia for herself. Inside the van it looks like Lassie's yard sale. Fancy water bowls in a cooler. Silver platters stacked in an Amazon box. A wreath as big around as a car tire. A bone-shaped cutting board. Laura and Judi take out one prize and pass it back and forth, trying to figure out if it does anything.

"That's South Carolina," Judi says.

"Yeah," Laura says. "But I'm not sure what it *is*, you know?"

There are also more personalized gifts. There's a portrait of Striker, and a second painting that looks like an ordinary field until you notice the artist painted Striker's face into one of the clouds. Laura and Judi stare at that one for a second.

"But wait! There's more," Laura says.

She reaches into the van and pulls out four long plastic bins, the kind you might slide under the bed to stash winter sweaters. They hold Striker's ribbons. So many ribbons. All the Best in

Shows, plus the breed and group ribbons for those shows, plus all the secondary ribbons from the shows he didn't win.

They take some of the stash into Betty White's living room to sort through. Judi has a box balanced on her lap when Striker wanders in and props his front feet on the cushion next to her, looking inside the box.

"Did you do that?" Judi says. "Did you do all that?"

The brilliant singer/songwriter Jason Isbell has a song called "If We Were Vampires." He is singing to a lover about the heartbreak of knowing their time together will not be eternal. Life comes with an expiration date. "Maybe we'll get forty years together," Isbell sings. "But one day I'll be gone, or one day you'll be gone."

Dogs and people never get forty years. The oldest dog in recorded history, according to Guinness World Records, was Bobi, a Rafeiro do Alentejo* from Portugal, who died in October 2023 at age thirty-one. That, of course, is at the far edge of the graph. The average dog lives ten to thirteen years, taking into account that you might not believe there is any such thing as an average dog.

Theologists still debate whether dogs go to heaven. In 2014, news reports announced that Pope Francis had settled the issue, at least as far as Catholics were concerned: "One day, we will see our animals again in the eternity of Christ. Paradise is open to all of God's creatures." But it turned out he was misquoted: An earlier

---

*Rafeiro do Alentejo: Also known as the Portuguese mastiff, originating from the Alentejo region of the country. ("Rafeiro" translates roughly as "mutt.") Bred to protect sheep and other livestock on the trips from summer to winter pastures. AKC description: "powerful, rustic, sober and calm."

pope had said that to a distraught child, and an Italian newspaper had concluded that something Francis said agreed with it, and the whole thing got so confusing and messy that the *New York Times* published a correction that ran to 223 words. It seems to me that if there is a heaven, dogs would be in it, because heaven is where we go for eternal happiness. Heaven is a place where your dog lives forever and never pees on the rug. But as much as some of us believe in the afterlife, there is no way to be sure. The only time we know we have is here. The days go slow but the years go fast. We had more than fourteen years with Fred—somewhere north of five thousand days—and sometimes the time with him feels like a brief gust of wind through our lives. We were too busy, too focused on work. We didn't always appreciate the miracle right in front of us.

Laura knows dogs as well as just about anybody in the world. She has spent her life in Dogland evaluating, analyzing, calculating—but also feeling, intuiting, connecting. So many dogs have flowed through her life. She knows exactly how special Striker is. Their time together was intense and wonderful and oh so short. Two years, eight months. Sometimes that is all the time you get.

Marc and Correen arrive in the early afternoon, backing their Expedition up to Betty White.

Laura comes out to give them a hug. It's a bit of an awkward moment. They can't do the handoff right away because she has to show other dogs first. Marc and Correen go over to watch the show and talk to Judi. They are used to the environment, and by now I am used to it, too. The details are a little different every time, but the scene is the same: the RVs, the grooming tables, the merch stand, the booth selling specialty dog treats. And in the middle of it all, the show rings: five or six going at once, circles bordering circles, all these dogs and all these people spending whatever time they have together.

A lot of the regulars have camp chairs with custom embroidered backs celebrating their kennel or their champion dog. Judi's chair says:

STRIKER

Samoyed

100 AKC Best In Shows

"It's a little outdated now," she says.

We're all killing time until the handoff. I ask Marc and Correen what it's like to own a dog that doesn't live with you. By now they've been through this lots of times. What might be strange to someone outside the fancy isn't strange to them at all.

"It's like sending your kid away, right?" Correen says.

"It's like if your kid goes back to university," Marc says.

"They always come back."

"It's not like they've gone. You're in touch, you go to shows."

Marc talks about how Striker has given them so many "pinch-me moments": the trips to the Garden, the breed and group wins at Westminster, those times when they allowed themselves to think he might win at all. They are proud of him and thrilled with what he and Laura did together. They also think he will be just fine being a normal dog. They've got a Siberian husky bitch named Awesome that Correen calls his "girlfriend"—not in the breeding sense, but just as buddies. It's not the show life, but it's a good life. Dogs adapt.

After a while they go back and gather outside the RV. Robin gives them a quick briefing on taking care of Striker. Here's the medicine he takes. Treats are easy—he loves everything. Trey Behm, one of Laura and Robin's assistants, brings Correen a Ziploc bag full of Striker's food. He likes to be fed at the same times every day, Trey says, so set alarms on your watch. He'll yip if you don't feed him on time. "Gonna be weird taking those alarms off," Trey says.

While the discussion is going on outside, Striker climbs into the cab of Betty White and takes the passenger seat. It's not a place he normally gets to be. For a minute he looks down at the people talking about him, just a couple of feet outside the passenger door. But then he turns and looks straight ahead, through the windshield. It's that calm stare I've seen from him so often. The dog show is happening over to his left, but he doesn't even glance that way. His sight is aimed out over the cornfields. I have no idea what he sees.

Eventually Robin goes inside the RV, and a few minutes later Laura returns from the show ring. She grabs a lead and climbs the steps. Robin is just on the other side of the door, hugging Striker, crying.

"Well," Laura says, "I was fine until I saw you."

Still, she holds it together as they step outside. She takes Striker to the ex-pen for one last pee. Then she walks him over to Marc and Correen's SUV. Everyone else stands back, as if they know this is not their moment.

The liftgate of the SUV is open. Awesome, the Siberian husky, is curled up in a crate on one side. The crate on the other side already has Striker's name on it. Laura reaches down and roughs his fur. He leans into her leg. She opens the crate and steps to the side so he can jump in.

Instead, he sits down.

Laura waves Striker toward the crate.

He does nothing.

She reaches between his shoulder blades, nudges him a little.

He doesn't move.

Now Laura is crying. She's also laughing. She is smart enough to see the layers here. She spent two and a half years training Striker to do what she says, and now he won't do anything. But also: they spent two and a half years together, and now she's sending him away. This is not Laura's car. This is not Laura's dog.

He can never speak the words. But everybody there knows what he is saying.

"Come on," Laura says, her eyes bright, the tears running. "Don't do this to me, you little shit."

She gives him one more moment.

He doesn't move.

So she scoops him up and puts him in the crate. Closes the crate door and lowers the liftgate. Turns to the little group standing nearby and shrugs.

Nobody is sure what to say, so they do a round of hugs. Marc and Correen get in the Expedition and Marc cranks it up. He rolls his window down. "There should be trumpets or something," he says. And then they drive off.

A few minutes ago Striker had been in the front of the RV, looking forward. Now he is in the rear of the SUV, looking back.

We watch until the SUV turns a corner and disappears.

Two years, eight months.

I turn to Laura, but she is already walking toward the rings. She still has work to do. Her show isn't over.

10

THE MAGIC TRICK

Most nights, before I close my eyes, I hear a ruckus out there in the leaves, hear that urgent bark, and I stumble out the door, to rescue some innocent possum, or treed cat, or just to poke my head out the door so he will see me and know that I have registered his diligence, that I have entered it into whatever ledger it is he thinks I keep; he just knows for sure there is one.

—Rick Bragg, *The Speckled Beauty*

A parade of Airedales circled the ring at the National Dog Show outside Philadelphia, and I was concentrating on them hard. I had found one of the rare folding chairs at ringside. I was taking notes, watching close, feeling stressed. My mind rolled down two tracks. Track one was capturing the moment: what it looked like (vast gray convention hall), smelled like (powdery, vague notes of dog funk underneath), sounded like (trimmed paws shuffling across the floor like brushes on a drumhead). Track two was pondering the subtext, the question I had set out on this journey into Dogland to answer: *Are show dogs happy?*

As I thought about it, I felt a strange pressure in the crook of my left arm.

Quick panic check: Not a heart attack. The pressure wasn't from the inside out. It was from the outside in. I looked down and saw a massive wet snout poking through the gap between my arm and my hip.

It belonged to a Bernese mountain dog, one of the giants of the Working Group, a sweet brute that can top 110 pounds. Behind me, its handler was apologizing and pulling back on the lead. At dog shows they have rules for approaching a dog, but it's not as clear what to do when a dog approaches you. I wasn't sure whether I had accidentally violated Dogland etiquette. But the Bernese seemed insistent. So I told the handler it was fine. She gave the dog some slack, and I wrapped my arm around its neck, and it rested its chin on my thigh. Two big galoots, just hanging out.

The dog stayed there for maybe half a minute, long enough that the handler started checking her phone. Then it pulled its head back through the hole, like a birth in reverse, and trotted off down the concourse. It left me a present: a wide smear of slobber on my khakis. Which made me laugh. Which was just what I needed.

I don't know what that moment was. Maybe something about me smelled good. Maybe I seemed like a guy who would have a cookie. Maybe I just looked like someone who needed a friend.

All I can tell you is what I believe. One, for those thirty seconds, I believe we were both happy and at peace. And two, I believe I'll remember those thirty seconds for as long as I remember anything.

• • •

Are show dogs happy? Even knowing all the unknowns, I think so. In all my visits to dog shows, I never saw a dog that looked miserable. I had worried that once I got behind the scenes, I'd see dogs being mistreated like peons being yelled at by an evil CEO. I had also worried that I'd run into zombie dogs who were medicated or brainwashed into submission. About the worst I saw was a couple of dogs who looked bored with the lack of action, like they'd rather be chasing a rabbit somewhere. By and large the dogs acted like normal creatures who just happened to have a certain talent, like the kid in elementary school who went on to sing on Broadway. Dogs like having a job and dog shows are steady work. I saw lots of stressed handlers and groomers, but I rarely saw a stressed show dog. It was like hanging out with furry monks.

At a show in Tennessee a couple of years ago I sat at a picnic table to interview Angela Lloyd, one of the best pro handlers. At the time she was showing Claire, a Scottish deerhound bitch named after the main character in the steamy time-travel drama *Outlander.* The name is a good fit; Claire the deerhound is a gorgeous creature, long-legged and elegant. But what really struck me about her was what she did while Angela and I talked. Which was . . . nothing. We spent forty-five minutes at that picnic table, and Claire just stood there watching us, panting softly, as if she was enjoying our company but was too shy to speak up.

I asked Angela what Claire gets out of being a show dog. Angela thought for a second. Attention, she said. Claire likes attention. She likes being treated like a queen.

And what does Angela get out of being a handler? Friendships. Plus the love of a special dog, like Claire. "I get up every morning for the dog," she said.

Claire was a real champion, winner of the National Dog Show two years in a row. But at the same time, there in Tennessee, she gave off no vibes of stress. Her eyes didn't wander. She looked at me sometimes and at Angela most of the time and seemed perfectly content to be where she was. When the interview was done and Angela stood up, Claire came over and nuzzled her leg, and they walked away at the same practiced pace.

Happy together.

Happiness is a slippery thing. Sometimes we're happy and don't know why. Sometimes we expect to be happy and aren't. Sometimes happiness feels like a distant star, a pinprick in the sky we can never reach. Sometimes we feel immersed in it, like the water of a warm pool.

I traveled Dogland wondering if show dogs are happy, and beyond that, if regular dogs are happy, too. But along the way I wandered into a different question: What does it take to make *us* happy?

That's the thing dogs, more than any other creatures on Earth, have figured out. Dogs can soften the hearts of misanthropes and bring timid folks out of their shells. They inspire poems and songs and books and movies and paintings and sculptures. They are able to reach inside and find the best of us in ways even other humans often can't.

It is such a normal thing now that we take it for granted. Two vastly different animals. One on two legs, one on four. No common spoken language. And yet, somehow, companions and friends. It is nature's greatest magic trick. We still have only the vaguest sense of how it was done. But a magic trick, like a recipe, has ingredients. And this magic trick has at least two.

• • •

The longer I spent in Dogland, the more I thought about treats.

The treat is Dogland's official currency. A treat can take many forms. Some show dogs are picky, but most are omnivores. They devour bits and chunks of whatever their handlers offer: ham, turkey, roast beef, chicken, salmon, hot dogs, liver, gizzards, pretty much any type of cheese. A show dog could crush the keto diet. I met a woman at a North Carolina show whose dog gobbled treats made from nutria, the giant hideous Louisiana swamp rat.

As with so many things, there is a double standard when it comes to treats. Male dog handlers have it easier because their clothes come with so many pockets. Women sometimes have to resort to stuffing theirs down the bra. Handlers of both sexes sometimes cram treats between cheek and gum like a dip of Copenhagen. Some handlers swear their dogs prefer it that way, warm and wet. However they do it, treats are essential. A handler never steps into the ring without them.

Among the fancy, treats are called bait. Baiting a dog means holding out the promise of a treat as incentive. A handler might hold out bait at the right height to get a dog into a natural stack. Other times a handler will throw bait eight or ten feet away, having trained the dog to freeze on the spot until the handler gives the OK to go get it. This is a common trick so dogs will hold a pose for a judge, or even for the photographers who take countless pictures of every winner at every show. (The photogs also deploy the occasional squeaky toy.)

In many ways the dog-show world runs on treats. A dog's goal—or one of them—is to end the day with a full belly. A handler's goal—or one of them—is to accumulate success and its signifiers. Treats serve both sides of the equation. Sometimes we laugh at the hoops a dog will jump through (sometimes literally) for a treat. But we're hoop jumpers, too. We work weekends in hopes of a bonus. We hit the gym all week to earn a cheat meal. We endure awkward first-date talk for a lingering kiss at the end. Treats are powerful incentives to be better versions of ourselves. They reward our little victories.

Treats also salve our losses. What happens when someone dies? People bring food. It's a gift of sustenance, a sign of love and support in the hardest times. We need treats in our worst moments as much or more as we do in our best. My mom, near the end of her life, craved ice cream. My brother lived nearby and would drive over to the nursing home to take her a little cup of Ben & Jerry's every night. When my wife and I were in town, we'd do the honors. The joy she got from that ice cream . . . it brought the rest of us joy, too.

At just about every dog show I went to, there were little bowls at the entrance to every ring and at the main table where you could pick up a show catalog. The bowls always had some kind of candy: Halloween-sized chocolate bars, Jolly Ranchers. Sometimes there'd be a tray with packs of peanut butter crackers or little bags of chips. I suppose some overworked handlers made a lunch out of those things on an especially harried day. But for most everybody else it was just a nice little ping of pleasure, something to carry us over to the next segment of the day.

One of the things we search for in life is someone, or something, that we can count on to provide us treats. A marriage, a friendship, a loving parent and child—one way to see those relationships is as a series of treats, given and received. The treat is not just the currency of Dogland. The treat is the currency of happiness.

Dogs and people learned this truth. It is possible they learned it together.

There is a second ingredient. Years ago my friend Chris Jones wrote a piece for *Esquire* magazine about Teller, the silent partner in the brilliant magic duo Penn & Teller. Teller speaks when he's not onstage, and he said something in the story that I have never forgotten:

"Sometimes magic is just someone spending more time on something than anyone else might reasonably expect."

Consider the experiment between people and dogs, the one that started when the wolf first lingered by the fire.

That—or something like it—happened at least fifteen thousand years ago. I'm not sure what gem or precious metal is appropriate for a fifteen thousandth anniversary. Unobtainium, maybe.

What happened over all that time? We're used to telling the story through the human point of view. We managed to take that one curious wolf and turn it into a remarkable array of breeds and crossbreeds and undefinable mixes—a family tree that looks like a maple grafted onto an oak grafted onto a rosebush. It is a remarkable trick in and of itself. But it has always required massive chunks of time. Even now breeders need dozens of generations before they get from the dogs they have to the dogs they want.

But think about it from the dogs' POV, as they grew and changed with every new litter. Part of evolution is learning your environment. It only makes sense that as breeders shaped dogs for one purpose or another, those evolutionary survivors also picked up on how to deal with people. It turns out that beyond the basics—food, sex, a safe place to sleep—dogs and humans both need affection, companionship, something they can think of as love. Do dogs love us? We might never know for sure. But at the very minimum they have learned to act like they love us. And that's good enough.

Their adaptive skills are one reason dogs became our closest partners in the animal world. They cope with not just new surroundings but new roles. Do you need someone to protect a junkyard? Learn a circus act? Comfort a dying child? Dogs can do that. And now they're our constant companions, having burrowed into our lives in every way but blood. They developed those skills over all those thousands of years that humans were tweaking their genes. We thought we were just making tools. It turned out we were building a family.

All this made me think about the "Sammy smile"—the upturned corners of the mouth that Striker and other Samoyeds have, but most dogs don't. I mentioned earlier that scientists believe Samoyeds evolved that way to keep their drool from dripping down and freezing to their faces in the Siberian winter. In other words, they adapted to survive. But that smile has also helped them in a different way—it warms a dog lover's heart. It's possible Samoyeds have edged out less popular breeds simply because they always look like they're happy to see us.

There's a fantastic scene toward the end of the movie *Absence of Malice* where an assistant attorney general, played by Wilford Brimley, convenes a group in a conference room. He's trying to

untangle a convoluted scheme supposedly set into action by a character played by Paul Newman. The fates of several powerful people
hang in the balance. At one point, after walking through part of the
scheme, Brimley turns to Newman and says: "Are you that smart?"

Are dogs that smart? Did they figure out, over thousands of
years, not just how to keep living but how to become indispensable to humans? And, in fact, is becoming indispensable to humans the way they figured out how to keep living?

*Sometimes magic is just someone spending more time on
something than anyone else might reasonably expect.*

Treats plus time equals magic.

It's more important than any equation Einstein discovered. It's
the formula that anchors all our relationships. It's the paperwork
of love.

Dog owners perform the magic trick every day and never even
think about it.

They might notice how fast the Milk-Bones disappear from
the box. They might glance at the clock and realize they've spent
the last hour playing tug-of-war with their hound. But they don't
think about the equation.

I just happened to spend the last few years watching how it
played out between people and dogs. I met Michelle Parris, weep-
ing with sadness about the dogs she had lost and with joy about
the dogs she still had, those little Italian greyhounds the through-
line in her life. I talked to Tressie McMillan Cottom, whose Havanese became not just a reward for her success but a reality that
knocked her sideways.

And I watched Laura and Striker together.

I saw Laura bow down to Striker so many times. It was a part of their routine. Right before she took him on a trip around the ring, she would bend over and cup his chin in her hand and say a couple of words or just make a *chk-chk* noise.

Other times she knelt. This happened a lot while they waited for the judge to look at another dog. She'd get down on one knee like a batter in the on-deck circle and comb any stray spots of fur, or spritz him with water, or turn on the portable fan.

We get down on dog level all the time without thinking much about what it means. It's giving up the position of dominance. It is treating the dog, just for a moment, as our equal. It's what all of us want, in this uneven world. Just to be able to stand on level ground.

And as we level dogs off, they do the same for us. We live in a word that can feel painful and unfair. Some days the whole human experiment feels doomed. But if there is a dog to come home to, or even watch in a park, it can remind us that there is still such beauty in the world, and still a path to happiness.

There are many sins we have to answer for in the way we have manipulated dogs over our history together. We still commit some of those sins. Shelters are full to overflowing with unwanted dogs. Puppy mills still mistreat mother dogs and their babies. Laboratories still use dogs for experiments. In many ways, the story of people and dogs is one long string of mixed messages.

But we have spent more time with dogs than any other creature on Earth, and they have spent more time with us. The cliché would be to say we were made for each other, but that's not quite it. We made each other, for each other. Humans created dogs, and dogs shaped humanity. They would not be here at all without us, and we would not be the same without them.

I think a lot about a particular Penn & Teller trick, one I saw them perform at their theater in Vegas. They call the trick Honor System. There were two boxes—one clear, with a lid like a shoebox, and a larger box made of wood with a hinged lid. Teller climbed into the clear box, and then assistants put him into the wooden box and locked it. There seemed to be no way Teller could get the lid off the clear box—the fit inside the wooden box was too tight. It looked impossible to escape.

Penn then announced that Teller would, in fact, escape. Not only that, Penn said, but they would give the audience a choice. He would start playing a song, and by the end of the song Teller would make his way out of the box and join him. If anybody in the audience wanted to see how it was done, all they had to do was keep their eyes open. If they didn't want to know, they could close their eyes.

I kept my eyes open.

I'm not going to spoil the trick here. But what I will say is that to me, knowing how the trick was done was even more breathtaking than being fooled. It took Penn & Teller more than twenty years to perfect that trick. All the work and the thought and the sweat that went into those few minutes onstage. Not to mention all the abandoned tricks that never made it there. So much time for that one treat. But it was worth it for the magic.

I asked Laura once how her life as a dog handler compares with how she had dreamed of it.

She laughed and said, "I'm an idiot."

Then she stopped and started again, wanting to give a better answer.

"I knew what I thought all the highs would be. I don't think I was prepared for how hard some of the lows would be."

She hadn't been prepared for juggling all the personalities of the dogs she worked with and the clients she worked for. She hadn't been prepared for when her dogs got sick. She definitely hadn't been prepared for when their time was done and she had to send them back home.

She hadn't been prepared for losing when she thought she had the better dog.

But she met Robin, the love of her life, out here in Dogland. She has made so many friends. She has built a career and earned respect and seen the world, even if "the world" sometimes meant a Residence Inn on a Saturday night. Mainly, she has spent time with dogs. Some people get only two or three dogs in their lives. Laura has had hundreds. And the best ones, the ones like Striker, take her back to the first dog she ever knew. Her mother bought Dora, that Belgian sheepdog, all those years ago. The seller had one condition: they had to take it to dog shows. So that's what Laura's mother did, and that set the path for Laura's life.

Laura learned to walk by holding on to Dora's tail. In all the ways that matter, she has never let go.

Epilogue

It is fall 2023, a little more than a year after Striker's retirement. According to his Facebook page, he keeps busy. There he is relaxing on Halloween, getting a checkup at the vet, going on a walk, curled up on the floor with Correen. He has become Awesome's trailing spouse. He follows her around the house in case she wants to play. "He's doing great," Correen says.

He had an orbit or two of fame after Westminster. The *New York Times Magazine* profiled him, his face and white fur filling the whole front cover. The headline: "Striker Will Never Know He Wasn't Best in Show."

He was a clue on *Jeopardy!*. As his picture appeared on the screen, host Ken Jennings gave the clue: "Seen here is Striker, a type of this Russian-named dog that won Westminster's title in 2022 for best Working Group dog." One contestant guessed "husky." Another guessed "Bolshoi," which is a ballet company, not a dog.

Laura and Robin went to Toronto to see him in the summer. It was part of a trip to see the singer/songwriter Pink. Laura and Robin love Pink almost as much as they love dogs. A few months before the Toronto trip, they had taken some vacation time to see a different Pink concert—her headlining show at Ohana Fest, a music festival south of Los Angeles. It was around the time of Robin's birthday, and they had been talking about getting married. Laura decided that would be the weekend. She called a friend who agreed to get ordained. The idea was for it to be a casual ceremony on Laguna Beach. But when they got there, Laura discovered their friends had made it into an Event, complete with a selection of wedding gowns for both of them. Laura told Robin at five in the morning that they were getting married that afternoon. They went to the concert the next night.

Robin is handling the top dog in their stable right now, an English springer spaniel named Freddie (full name: GCHS CH Telltale Bohemian Rhapsody). He's the number three dog in the country. Laura is still looking for the next Striker. She knows she might never find another.

"There's a part of you that is more guarded when you do this job," she says. "You know your time together is relatively short. But, yeah, there's an empty place now that we're not working together. I do miss him."

She takes a long breath.

"Significantly."

One afternoon, watching Striker run the ring at a show, I thought of another question: *How much of this will he remember?*

It's hard to tell exactly what dogs remember, and why. Some studies show that a dog's short-term memory lasts only a couple of minutes. That's one reason we talk about dogs living in the moment. It's one of the gifts they give us—the reminder that we should always approach the world as fresh and new.

But dogs obviously retain longer memories, too—what scientists generally call associative memories. If you ever pull a treat from your jeans pocket, a dog will keep sticking its nose in there just in case you have another one.

What's not as clear is whether dogs have episodic memory, which is less connective and more abstract. Does a dog remember that day it went for a hike in the mountains? Does it remember the day someone rescued it from the pound? Does a dog do what we do: connect the dots of a life and make a story?

In 2008, I had surgery to remove a benign tumor from my heart. That's not nearly as bad as it sounds, but it was, briefly, open heart surgery. So I was laid up at home for a while afterward. I spent most of my day in a chair in the living room with Fred hanging out a few feet away in his dog bed. Alix's parents came from Tennessee to help her, and the three of them would often work in the back of the house while I dozed. Friends would stop by all day long with food and drinks and hugs and gossip. I could see them coming up the sidewalk, but I couldn't get up to answer the door. And I didn't want them to ring our ancient doorbell, which startled the hell out of all of us—it sounded like the buzzer at a high-school basketball game. So I would holler, "Hey, Alix!" and she would race to the door to open it. And Fred would jump up and run to the door with her.

Not long after the surgery, we went to Boston for a year on a fellowship. Months after we got back—at least a year and a half after the surgery—I was in the living room one day and needed to ask Alix something. She was in our office in the back. I hollered, "Hey, Alix!"

And Fred jumped up and ran to the door.

There's no way of knowing the memory map in his brain that led him to do that. Maybe it was a simple conditioned response, like Pavlov's drooling dogs. Maybe it was just a sticky note that had lodged in his dog brain: Tommy, holler, Alix, door. But to us, the storytellers, it felt like a tale he remembered from long ago, one where he knew the ending. It sure felt like a story to Alix and me. Fifteen years later we still talk about it.

Marc and Correen tell a story, too. When they take Striker for a walk and they run into somebody on the street, he freezes into place.

He's not scared.

He's forming a stack.

You can see that as an associative memory—here's a stranger, maybe it's a dog show judge, better shape up. But you can also choose to believe it as a dog telling a story. *This is what I used to be.*

Striker, whether he knows it or not, is in the business of creating memories. He just happened to have a few years in Dogland creating them for the public. When people saw him, they felt something. Maybe they laughed at that incredible white fur, or they cheered for him against the little yappy dogs, or they longed for someone like him as a companion, a presence, a friend.

This is part of our unspoken pact with the dog. Make memories for us. Give us stories to tell.

Laura King can tell Striker stories for the rest of her life. She will remember him as long as she will remember anything. He was her champion and her heart-dog, and he gave her that feeling she had been searching for since she was a little girl.

That feeling has a lot of names, but the shorthand is happiness.

There are so many ways to tell the story of dogs and their people. The story goes back so far, and there are so many things we don't know. I mentioned earlier on how dogs are like movie screens we project our own lives onto. When you tell a dog story, it's hard to tell the story *about* the dog. Instead you tell the story *through* the dog. The dog is the medium to tell a story about people. And the story is about the whole history of humanity: from a dog show in the current moment, back through dogs as house pets, back again through dogs as tools, all the way back to when there were no dogs at all, and one night a wolf crept a little closer to the fire.

There are gaps in that story, and the biggest gaps we cannot fill because we cannot quote one of the main sources. Dogs have left no artworks on cave walls, no runes to interpret, no scrolls to discover, no voluminous journals. The inner life of a dog might forever be as enigmatic as the Sammy smile.

Science may one day be able to measure not just what a dog remembers but what those memories mean to the dog. Until then we have to rely on what we can see, and what we choose to believe.

One way to make the story make sense is this: we long for happiness and dogs long for happiness, and we found it in each other, and we put up with all the rest just to hold on to that one precious thing.

We remember this, generation after generation, and somehow dogs sense it, too.

So. If Striker remembers the stack, what else does he remember? Ponder it long enough and you can make yourself believe he remembers it all: the rides between towns, the hotel snuggles, the combing and spraying, the strangers checking his teeth, the smell of the Hudson River, the feel of his feet on dirt and concrete and grass. The other dogs, so many. All those little walks, around the ring, down and back, under the lights.

The woman by his side.

Acknowledgments

Every book is a ship trying to get to port, and the writer at the wheel is often about two paragraphs away from steering the damn thing into the rocks. It takes a whole crew to guide the vessel home.

Thanks to my agent, Sloan Harris, for always being a fan and always telling the truth at the same time. That's a gift not many have. Thanks to Jofie Ferrari-Adler of Avid Reader, who has edited both my books with enthusiasm and kindness and skill. We went through a bunch of book ideas this time around and he picked this one out of the stash from a one-line summary. I'm so lucky to work with someone with that kind of vision.

Evan Gaffney designed the gorgeous book jacket. Ruth Lee-Mui did the interior design. Jessica Chin, the copyediting manager, and Nicole Bruger-Dethmers, copy editor, smoothed out my wrinkled manuscript. My words have never looked better than they have in their hands. Rhina Garcia did the publicity, Caroline McGregor handled the marketing, and they've both been a joy to work with. Carolyn Kelly made sure all these different pieces were aimed in the same direction.

It's a huge commitment to read a book draft *and* give useful feedback. Deep thanks to the early readers who did just that: Kim

Cross, Bronwen Dickey, Mary Fluke, Joe Posnanski, and Rachel Robertson. They saved my bacon multiple times and brought the book into clearer focus.

So many people in the dog-show world were gracious and generous—especially Gail Miller Bisher, Ryan Boyko, David Frei, Angela Lloyd, Michelle Parris, Stephanie Parker, Lisa Peterson, Justin and Cheslie Smithey, Roxanne Sutton, and Emma-Jean Weinstein.

Tressie McMillan Cottom, Josh Dawsey, and Scott Van Pelt took time out of their bustling lives to talk to me about their dogs, although I didn't have to twist their arms too hard. Alexandra Horowitz and Hal Herzog were among the many dog experts who helped me understand what we know (and still don't know) about what dogs think and feel.

Thanks to the readers of my newsletter, *The Writing Shed*, for putting up with the six hundred and ninety-four times I encouraged them to BUY THE BOOK. And thanks to my colleagues at WFAE for giving me the flexibility to write it, and for allowing me to be a small part of a great team.

I wrote a lot of this book in coffeeshops all over Charlotte—shoutout to Mugs, Summit Coffee, Amelie's, Common Market, and the Giddy Goat for giving me refuge and caffeine.

My greatest stroke of luck in doing this book was meeting Laura King. She is funny, frank, insightful, easy to talk to, and so damn good at her job. May she and Robin be blessed with great seats for Pink from here to eternity. Thanks to everyone else at Daybreak Kennels. Thanks to Judi Elford, Correen Pacht, and Mark Ralsky, who helped me understand their investment in Striker's life, financially and emotionally.

Striker! Hey there. Good boy.

Just as I started reporting this book, my mother-in-law moved in with us. That's not the setup for a joke—it's the description of a delight. Joann Felsing has been a daily joy in our lives, and also endless entertainment. Thank you for coming to stay with us, and yes, there's more ice cream in the fridge.

Love to all our family members, on the Felsing side and the Tomlinson side. Please come visit. Because when you do, that's when we clean the house.

The best for last: Alix Felsing handles this crazy life we've built with courage, kindness, and love. I don't always know where it comes from, and I don't always think I deserve it, but I always know it's there. We fill each other up.

Recommended Reading

"Books are made out of books," Cormac McCarthy once said. He called that an "ugly fact," but I think it's sort of beautiful. Every new book springs from the soil of books that came before. Here are some of the books that helped make this one.

The Dog Show by William F. Stifel (2003): The authoritative history of the Westminster Dog Show.

Best in Show by Bo Bengston (2008): A deep and rich look (more than 600 pages) at how dog shows began and how they work. If you have any interest in showing a dog, here's where you start.

Show Dog by Josh Dean (2012): The dog-show world, told through the eyes of an Australian shepherd named Jack and his people.

Our Dogs, Ourselves by Alexandra Horowitz (2019): Horowitz is the best modern writer on dogs and how they see the world. This book, which centers on the relationship between dogs and people, is my favorite of hers.

Some We Love, Some We Hate, Some We Eat by Hal Herzog (2010): A thoughtful and realistic look at how and why we treat some animals (especially dogs) so much better than others.

The New Work of Dogs by Jon Katz (2003): A detailed look into how dogs' jobs have evolved from blue-collar work to caretaking and companionship.

What the Dog Knows by Cat Warren (2013): Warren trains her dog, Solo, to be a search dog—and along the way tells the story of how dogs perceive the world, and how people and dogs learn to work together.

Pit Bull by Bronwen Dickey (2017): A smart and thoroughly reported reevaluation of the world's most misunderstood dogs.

The Animal Estate by Harriet Ritvo (1989): An exploration of animals in the Victorian age, when dogs first started becoming pets of the working class.

Pets in America by Katherine C. Grier (2006): Similar to *The Animal Estate,* but told from the US perspective.

About the Author

TOMMY TOMLINSON is the author of the memoir *The Elephant in the Room*, about life as an overweight man in America. He's also host of the podcast *SouthBound* at WFAE, the NPR station in Charlotte, North Carolina. His newsletter is called *The Writing Shed with Tommy Tomlinson*. He lives in Charlotte with his wife, Alix Felsing; her mother, Joann Felsing; and their cat, Jack Reacher.